Go Standard Library Cookbook

Over 120 specific ways to make full use of the standard
library components in Golang

Radomír Sohlich

BIRMINGHAM - MUMBAI

Go Standard Library Cookbook

Commissioning Editor: Merint Mathew
Acquisition Editor: Aiswarya Narayanan
Content Development Editor: Anugraha Arunagiri
Technical Editor: Subhalaxmi Nadar
Copy Editor: Safis Editing
Project Coordinator: Ulhas Kambali
Proofreader: Safis Editing
Indexer: Rekha Nair
Graphics: Tania Dutta
Production Coordinator: Arvindkumar Gupta

First published: February 2018

Production reference: 1230218

Published by Packt Publishing Ltd.
Livery Place
35 Livery Street
Birmingham
B3 2PB, UK.

ISBN 978-1-78847-527-3

www.packtpub.com

`mapt.io`

Mapt is an online digital library that gives you full access to over 5,000 books and videos, as well as industry leading tools to help you plan your personal development and advance your career. For more information, please visit our website.

Why subscribe?

- Spend less time learning and more time coding with practical eBooks and Videos from over 4,000 industry professionals

- Improve your learning with Skill Plans built especially for you

- Get a free eBook or video every month

- Mapt is fully searchable

- Copy and paste, print, and bookmark content

PacktPub.com

Did you know that Packt offers eBook versions of every book published, with PDF and ePub files available? You can upgrade to the eBook version at `www.PacktPub.com` and as a print book customer, you are entitled to a discount on the eBook copy. Get in touch with us at `service@packtpub.com` for more details.

At `www.PacktPub.com`, you can also read a collection of free technical articles, sign up for a range of free newsletters, and receive exclusive discounts and offers on Packt books and eBooks.

Contributors

About the author

Radomír Sohlich received the master's degree in Applied Informatics from Faculty of Applied Informatics at Tomas Bata University in Zlín. After that, he got a job in a start-up company as a software developer and worked on various projects, usually based on the Java platform. Currently, he continues a software developer career as a contractor for a large international company.

In 2015, he fell in love with Go and kept exploring the endless power and possibilities of the language. He is passionate about learning new approaches and technology and feels the same about sharing the knowledge with others.

> *I'd like to thank my beloved wife and kids for the time they gave me for creating this book. The next big thank you belongs to Mert Serin, who agreed to review the book and give a feedback on the content.*

About the reviewer

Mert Serin was born in Izmir in 1993, graduated from Hacettepe University in 2016, and has worked on iOS development since his third year in university. He is currently working at USIT Inc., a start-up based in Atlanta, GE, as a full stack developer.

Packt is searching for authors like you

If you're interested in becoming an author for Packt, please visit `authors.packtpub.com` and apply today. We have worked with thousands of developers and tech professionals, just like you, to help them share their insight with the global tech community. You can make a general application, apply for a specific hot topic that we are recruiting an author for, or submit your own idea.

Table of Contents

Preface   1

Chapter 1: Interacting with the Environment   7
Introduction   7
Retrieving the Golang version   8
    Getting ready   8
    How to do it...   8
    How it works...   9
Accessing program arguments   10
    How to do it...   10
    How it works...   11
    There's more…   11
Creating a program interface with the flag package   12
    How to do it...   12
    How it works...   14
    There's more…   15
Getting and setting environment variables with default values   15
    How to do it…   15
    How it works…   18
Retrieving the current working directory   19
    How to do it...   19
    How it works…   20
Getting the current process PID   21
    How to do it…   21
    How it works…   22
Handling operating system signals   22
    How to do it…   23
    How it works…   24
Calling an external process   25
    Getting ready   25
    How to do it…   26

How it works…	28
See also	29
Retrieving child process information	29
Getting ready	29
How to do it…	29
How it works…	32
See also	32
Reading/writing from the child process	32
Getting ready	32
How to do it…	33
How it works…	39
Shutting down the application gracefully	40
How to do it…	40
How it works…	43
See also	43
File configuration with functional options	43
How to do it…	43
How it works…	46
Chapter 2: Strings and Things	47
Introduction	47
Finding the substring in a string	48
How to do it…	48
How it works…	49
See also	49
Breaking the string into words	50
How to do it…	50
How it works…	53
There's more…	54
Joining the string slice with a separator	54
How to do it…	54
How it works…	56
There's more…	57
Concatenating a string with writer	57
How to do it…	57
How it works…	59

There's more...   59
Aligning text with tabwriter   60
   How to do it...   61
   How it works...   62
Replacing part of the string   62
   How to do it...   62
   How it works...   64
   There's more...   65
Finding the substring in text by the regex pattern   65
   How to do it...   65
   How it works...   66
   See also   67
Decoding a string from the non-Unicode charset   67
   How to do it...   67
   How it works...   69
Controlling case   70
   How to do it...   70
   How it works...   72
Parsing comma-separated data   72
   How to do it...   73
   How it works...   75
Managing whitespace in a string   76
   How to do it...   76
   How it works...   77
   See also   78
Indenting a text document   78
   How to do it...   79
   How it works...   80
   See also   80
Chapter 3: Dealing with Numbers   81
Introduction   81
Converting strings to numbers   82
   How to do it...   82
   How it works...   83
Comparing floating-point numbers   84

How to do it...   84
How it works...   86
Rounding floating-point numbers   87
How to do it...   87
How it works...   88
Floating-point arithmetics   89
How to do it...   89
How it works...   90
There's more...   90
See also   91
Formatting numbers   91
How to do it...   91
How it works...   93
There's more...   94
Converting between binary, octal, decimal, and hexadecimal   94
How to do it...   94
How it works...   96
Formatting with the correct plurals   96
Getting ready   96
How to do it...   96
How it works...   98
There's more...   98
Generating random numbers   99
How to do it...   99
How it works...   100
Operating complex numbers   101
How to do it...   101
How it works...   102
Converting between degrees and radians   103
How to do it...   103
How it works...   104
Taking logarithms   105
How to do it...   105
How it works...   106
Generating checksums   106

How to do it...   106
How it works...   109

Chapter 4: Once Upon a Time   111
Introduction   111
Finding today's date   112
How to do it...   112
How it works...   112
See also   113
Formatting date to string   113
How to do it...   113
How it works...   114
See also   115
Parsing the string into date   115
How to do it...   115
How it works...   117
Converting dates to epoch and vice versa   117
How to do it...   117
How it works...   118
Retrieving time units from the date   119
How to do it...   119
How it works...   120
Date arithmetics   120
How to do it...   120
How it works...   121
Finding the difference between two dates   122
How to do it...   122
How it works...   123
Converting between time zones   123
How to do it...   124
How it works...   125
Running the code block periodically   125
How to do it...   125
How it works...   126
Waiting a certain amount of time   127
How to do it...   127

How it works...   128
Timeout long-running operations   129
How to do it...   129
How it works...   130
There's more...   131
Serializing the time and date   131
How to do it...   131
How it works...   132

Chapter 5: In and Out   133
Introduction   133
Reading standard input   134
How to do it...   134
How it works...   137
Writing standard output and error   137
How to do it...   137
How it works...   139
Opening a file by name   139
How to do it...   139
How it works...   141
Reading the file into a string   141
How to do it...   141
How it works...   143
Reading/writing a different charset   143
How to do it...   143
How it works...   145
See also   145
Seeking a position within a file   145
How to do it...   145
How it works...   148
Reading and writing binary data   149
How to do it...   149
How it works...   150
Writing to multiple writers at once   151
How to do it...   151
How it works...   152

Piping between writer and reader 152
How to do it... 152
How it works... 153
Serializing objects to binary format 154
How to do it... 154
How it works... 156
Reading and writing ZIP files 156
How to do it... 156
How it works... 158
Parsing a large XML file effectively 159
How to do it... 159
How it works... 161
Extracting data from an incomplete JSON array 161
How to do it... 161
How it works... 163

Chapter 6: Discovering the Filesystem 165
Introduction 165
Getting file information 166
How to do it... 166
How it works... 167
Creating temporary files 167
How to do it... 167
How it works... 168
Writing the file 169
How to do it... 169
How it works... 170
Writing the file from multiple goroutines 170
How to do it... 170
How it works... 172
Listing a directory 172
How to do it... 172
How it works... 174
Changing file permissions 175
How to do it... 175
How it works... 176

Creating files and directories 176
How to do it... 176
How it works... 177
Filtering file listings 178
How to do it... 178
How it works... 179
See also 180
Comparing two files 180
How to do it... 180
How it works... 183
Resolving the user home directory 183
How to do it... 183
How it works... 184
Chapter 7: Connecting the Network 185
Introduction 185
Resolving local IP addresses 186
How to do it... 186
How it works... 187
Connecting to the remote server 188
How to do it... 188
How it works... 189
Resolving the domain by IP address and vice versa 190
How to do it... 190
How it works... 191
Connecting to the HTTP server 191
How to do it... 192
How it works... 194
See also 194
Parsing and building a URL 195
How to do it... 195
How it works... 196
Creating an HTTP request 196
How to do it... 196
How it works... 198
Reading and writing HTTP headers 198

How to do it...   199
How it works...   200
Handling HTTP redirects   200
How to do it...   201
How it works...   203
Consuming the RESTful API   203
How to do it...   203
How it works...   206
Sending a simple email   206
Getting ready   206
How to do it...   206
How it works...   208
Calling the JSON-RPC service   209
How to do it...   209
How it works...   211
Chapter 8: Working with Databases   213
Introduction   213
Connecting the database   214
Getting ready   214
How to do it...   214
How it works...   215
Validating the connection   216
Getting ready   216
How to do it...   216
How it works...   218
Executing statements   218
Getting ready   218
How to do it...   218
How it works...   221
Operations with prepared statements   221
Getting ready   221
How to do it...   221
How it works...   224
Canceling the pending query   225
Getting ready   225

How to do it...   225
How it works...   227
Reading query result metadata   228
Getting ready   228
How to do it...   228
How it works...   230
Retrieving data from a query result   231
Getting ready   231
How to do it...   231
How it works...   234
Parsing the query result into a map   234
Getting ready   234
How to do it...   234
How it works...   237
Handling transactions   238
Getting ready   238
How to do it...   238
How it works...   241
Executing stored procedures and functions   241
Getting ready   241
How to do it...   242
How it works...   243
Chapter 9: Come to the Server Side   245
Introduction   245
Creating the TCP server   246
How to do it...   246
How it works...   247
Creating the UDP server   248
How to do it...   248
How it works...   249
Handling multiple clients   250
How to do it...   250
How it works...   252
Creating the HTTP Server   252
How to do it...   252

How it works... 253

Handling HTTP requests 254
How to do it... 254
How it works... 255

Creating HTTP middleware layer 256
How to do it... 256
How it works... 257

Serving static files 258
How to do it... 258
How it works... 260

Serving content generated with templates 260
How to do it... 260
How it works... 261

Handling redirects 262
How to do it... 262
How it works... 263

Handling cookies 264
How to do it... 264
How it works... 266

Gracefully shutdown the HTTP server 267
How to do it... 267
How it works... 269

Serving secured HTTP content 269
Getting ready 269
How to do it... 270
How it works... 271

Resolving form variables 271
How to do it... 271
How it works... 272

Chapter 10: Fun with Concurrency 273
Introduction 273
Synchronizing access to a resource with Mutex 274
How to do it... 274
How it works... 276
Creating map for concurrent access 276

How to do it...	277
How it works...	278
Running a code block only once	278
How to do it...	279
How it works...	280
Pooling resources across multiple goroutines	281
How to do it...	281
How it works...	282
Synchronizing goroutines with WaitGroup	283
How to do it...	283
How it works...	284
Getting the fastest result from multiple sources	285
How to do it...	285
How it works...	287
Propagating errors with errgroup	287
How to do it...	288
How it works...	289
Chapter 11: Tips and Tricks	291
Introduction	291
Logging customization	292
How to do it...	292
How it works...	293
Testing the code	293
How to do it...	293
How it works...	295
See also	295
Benchmarking the code	295
How to do it...	295
How it works...	296
See also	297
Creating subtests	297
How to do it...	297
How it works...	298
See also	299
Testing the HTTP handler	299

How to do it... 299

How it works... 301

Accessing tags via reflection 301

How to do it... 301

How it works... 302

Sorting slices 302

How to do it... 303

How it works... 304

Breaking HTTP handlers into groups 304

How to do it... 305

How it works... 306

Utilizing HTTP/2 server push 307

Getting ready 307

How to do it... 307

How it works... 309

Other Books You May Enjoy 311

Index 315

Preface

Thanks for giving this book a chance! This book is a guide that takes you through the possibilities of the Go standard library, which has a lot of out-of-the-box functionality and solutions. Note that the solutions covered in the book are mainly simple demonstrations of how the standard library implementation is used and how it works. These recipes are meant to provide a starting point for you to work out how to solve your specific problem rather than solve the problem completely.

Who this book is for

This book is for those who want to strengthen the basics and reveal hidden parts of the Go standard library. The book expects readers to have the elementary knowledge of Go. For some recipes, a basic understanding of HTML, operating systems, and networking will be helpful.

What this book covers

Chapter 1, *Interacting with the Environment*, explores how your code can interact with the operating system environment. The use of command-line flags and arguments, consuming signals, and working with child processes are also covered.

Chapter 2, *Strings and Things*, goes through common operations on strings, from simple searching for substrings to formatting text to tabs.

Chapter 3, *Dealing with Numbers*, sheds light on basic conversions and number formatting options. Operations with large numbers and the correct use of plurals within output messages are covered.

Chapter 4, *Once Upon a Time*, puts the time package under the magnifying glass and covers formatting, arithmetics, and running code for given time period or after a certain delay.

Chapter 5, *In and Out*, covers I/O operations that utilize standard Go interfaces. Besides the basic I/O, the chapter also covers some useful serialization formats and how to handle them.

`Chapter 6`, *Discover the Filesystem*, discusses working with the filesystem, including listing the folders, reading and changing the file attributes, and comparing files side by side.

`Chapter 7`, *Connect the Network*, showcases the client-side implementations for connecting the TCP and UDP server, along with the use of SMTP, HTTP, and JSON-RPC .

`Chapter 8`, *Working with Databases*, focuses on common database tasks such as data selection and extraction, transaction handling and execution, and the shortcomings of stored procedures.

`Chapter 9`, *Come to the Server Side*, provides a view on networking from the server's perspective. TCP, UDP, and HTTP server basics are presented.

`Chapter 10`, *Fun with Concurrency*, deals with mechanisms of synchronization and concurrent access to resources.

`Chapter 11`, *Tips and Tricks*, comes with useful tips for testing and improving the HTTP server implementation and shows the benefits of HTTP/2 push.

To get the most out of this book

Although the Go programming platform is cross-platform, the recipes in the book usually assumes a Unix-based operating system, or at least that some common Unix utilities are available for execution. For Windows users, the Cygwin or GitBash utilities could be useful. The sample code works best with this setup:

- Unix-based environment
- A version of Go equal to or greater than 1.9.2
- An internet connection
- Read, write, and execute permissions on a folder where the sample code will be created and executed

Download the example code files

You can download the example code files for this book from your account at `www.packtpub.com`. If you purchased this book elsewhere, you can visit `www.packtpub.com/support` and register to have the files emailed directly to you.

You can download the code files by following these steps:

1. Log in or register at `www.packtpub.com`.
2. Select the **SUPPORT** tab.
3. Click on **Code Downloads & Errata**.
4. Enter the name of the book in the **Search** box and follow the onscreen instructions.

Once the file is downloaded, please make sure that you unzip or extract the folder using the latest version of:

- WinRAR/7-Zip for Windows
- Zipeg/iZip/UnRarX for Mac
- 7-Zip/PeaZip for Linux

The code bundle for the book is also hosted on GitHub at `https://github.com/PacktPublishing/Go-Standard-Library-Cookbook`. In case there's an update to the code, it will be updated on the existing GitHub repository.

We also have other code bundles from our rich catalog of books and videos available at `https://github.com/PacktPublishing/`. Check them out!

Conventions used

There are a number of text conventions used throughout this book.

`CodeInText`: Indicates code words in text, database table names, folder names, filenames, file extensions, pathnames, dummy URLs, user input, and Twitter handles. Here is an example: "Verify that your `GOPATH` and `GOROOT` environmental variables are set properly."

A block of code is set as follows:

```
package main
import (
  "log"
  "runtime"
)
```

When we wish to draw your attention to a particular part of a code block, the relevant lines or items are set in bold:

```
package main
import (
  "log"
  "runtime"
)
```

Bold: Indicates a new term, an important word, or words that you see onscreen. For example, words in menus or dialog boxes appear in the text like this.

Warnings or important notes appear like this.

Tips and tricks appear like this.

Sections

In this book, you will find several headings that appear frequently (*Getting ready*, *How to do it...*, *How it works...*, *There's more...*, and *See also*).

To give clear instructions on how to complete a recipe, use these sections as follows:

Getting ready

This section tells you what to expect in the recipe and describes how to set up any software or any preliminary settings required for the recipe.

How to do it...

This section contains the steps required to follow the recipe.

How it works...

This section usually consists of a detailed explanation of what happened in the previous section.

There's more...

This section consists of additional information about the recipe in order to make you more knowledgeable about the recipe.

See also

This section provides helpful links to other useful information for the recipe.

Get in touch

Feedback from our readers is always welcome.

General feedback: Email `feedback@packtpub.com` and mention the book title in the subject of your message. If you have questions about any aspect of this book, please email us at `questions@packtpub.com`.

Errata: Although we have taken every care to ensure the accuracy of our content, mistakes do happen. If you have found a mistake in this book, we would be grateful if you would report this to us. Please visit `www.packtpub.com/submit-errata`, selecting your book, clicking on the Errata Submission Form link, and entering the details.

Piracy: If you come across any illegal copies of our works in any form on the internet, we would be grateful if you would provide us with the location address or website name. Please contact us at `copyright@packtpub.com` with a link to the material.

If you are interested in becoming an author: If there is a topic that you have expertise in and you are interested in either writing or contributing to a book, please visit `authors.packtpub.com`.

Reviews

Please leave a review. Once you have read and used this book, why not leave a review on the site that you purchased it from? Potential readers can then see and use your unbiased opinion to make purchase decisions, we at Packt can understand what you think about our products, and our authors can see your feedback on their book. Thank you!

For more information about Packt, please visit `packtpub.com`.

1
Interacting with the Environment

In this chapter, the following recipes are covered:

- Retrieving the Golang version
- Accessing program arguments
- Creating a program interface with the flag package
- Getting and setting environment variables with default values
- Retrieving the current working directory
- Getting the current process PID
- Handling operating system signals
- Calling an external process
- Retrieving child process information
- Reading/writing from the child process
- Shutting down the application gracefully
- File configuration with functional options

Introduction

Every program, once it is executed, exists in the environment of the operating system. The program receives input and provides output to this environment. The operating system also needs to communicate with the program to let it know what's happening outside. And finally, the program needs to respond with appropriate actions.

This chapter will walk you through the basics of the discovery of the system environment, the program parameterization via program arguments, and the concept of the operating system signals. You will also learn how to execute and communicate with the child process.

Retrieving the Golang version

While building a program, it is a good practice to log the environment settings, build version, and runtime version, especially if your application is more complex. This helps you to analyze the problem, in case something goes wrong.

Besides the build version and, for example, the environmental variables, the Go version by which the binary was compiled could be included in the log. The following recipe will show you how to include the Go runtime version into such program information.

Getting ready

Install and verify the Go installation. The following steps could help:

1. Download and install Go on your machine.
2. Verify that your GOPATH and GOROOT environmental variables are set properly.
3. Open your Terminal and execute go version. If you get output with a version name, then Go is installed properly.
4. Create a repository in the GOPATH/src folder.

How to do it...

The following steps cover the solution:

1. Open the console and create the folder chapter01/recipe01.
2. Navigate to the directory.
3. Create the main.go file with the following content:

```
package main
import (
  "log"
  "runtime"
)
const info = `
```

```
   Application %s starting.
   The binary was build by GO: %s`

func main() {
   log.Printf(info, "Example", runtime.Version())
}
```

4. Run the code by executing the `go run main.go`.
5. See the output in the Terminal:

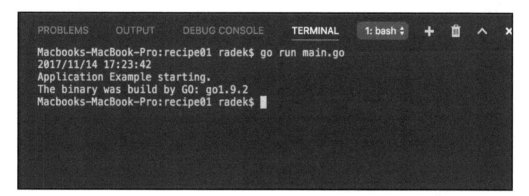

How it works...

The `runtime` package contains a lot of useful functions. To find out the Go runtime version, the `Version` function could be used. The documentation states that the function returns the hash of the commit, and the date or tag at the time of the binary build.

The `Version` function, in fact, returns the `runtime/internal/sys` .The `Version` constant. The constant itself is located in the `$GOROOT/src/runtime/internal/sys/zversion.go` file.

This `.go` file is generated by the `go dist` tool and the version is resolved by the `findgoversion` function in the `go/src/cmd/dist/build.go` file, as explained next.

The `$GOROOT/VERSION` takes priority. If the file is empty or does not exist, the `$GOROOT/VERSION.cache` file is used. If the `$GOROOT/VERSION.cache` is also not found, the tool tries to resolve the version by using the Git information, but in this case, you need to initialize the Git repository for the Go source.

Accessing program arguments

The most simple way to parameterize the program run is to use the command-line arguments as program parameters.

Simply, the parameterized program call could look like this: `./parsecsv user.csv role.csv`. In this case, `parsecsv` is the name of the executed binary and `user.csv` and `role.csv` are the arguments, that modify the program call (in this case it refers to files to be parsed).

How to do it...

1. Open the console and create the folder `chapter01/recipe02`.
2. Navigate to the directory.
3. Create the `main.go` file with the following content:

```
package main
import (
  "fmt"
  "os"
)

func main() {

  args := os.Args

  // This call will print
  // all command line arguments.
  fmt.Println(args)

  // The first argument, zero item from slice,
  // is the name of the called binary.
  programName := args[0]
  fmt.Printf("The binary name is: %s \n", programName)

  // The rest of the arguments could be obtained
  // by omitting the first argument.
  otherArgs := args[1:]
  fmt.Println(otherArgs)

  for idx, arg := range otherArgs {
    fmt.Printf("Arg %d = %s \n", idx, arg)
```

```
     }
   }
```

4. Build the binary by executing `go build -o test`.

5. Execute the command `./test arg1 arg2`. (Windows users can run `test.exe arg1 arg2`).

6. See the output in the Terminal:

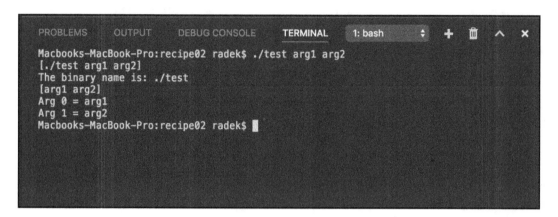

```
PROBLEMS    OUTPUT    DEBUG CONSOLE    TERMINAL    1: bash    ⬍    +    🗑    ∧    ✕
Macbooks-MacBook-Pro:recipe02 radek$ ./test arg1 arg2
[./test arg1 arg2]
The binary name is: ./test
[arg1 arg2]
Arg 0 = arg1
Arg 1 = arg2
Macbooks-MacBook-Pro:recipe02 radek$ █
```

How it works...

The Go standard library offers a few ways to access the arguments of the program call. The most generic way is to access the arguments by the `Args` variable from the OS package.

This way you can get all the arguments from the command line in a string slice. The advantage of this approach is that the number of arguments is dynamic and this way you can, for example, pass the names of the files to be processed by the program.

The preceding example just echoes all the arguments that are passed to the program. Finally, let's say the binary is called `test` and the program run is executed by the Terminal command `./test arg1 arg2`.

In detail, the `os.Args[0]` will return `./test`. The `os.Args[1:]` returns the rest of the arguments without the binary name. In the real world, it is better to not rely on the number of arguments passed to the program, but always check the length of the argument array. Otherwise, naturally, if the argument on a given index is not within the range, the program panics.

There's more...

If the arguments are defined as flags, `-flag value`, additional logic is needed to assign the value to the flag. In this case, there is a better way to parse these by using the `flag` package. This approach is part of the next recipe.

Creating a program interface with the flag package

The previous recipe describes how to access the program arguments by a very generic approach.

This recipe will provide a way of defining an interface via the program flags. This approach dominates systems based on GNU/Linux, BSD, and macOS. The example of the program call could be `ls -l` which will, on *NIX systems, list the files in a current directory.

The Go package for flag handling does not support flag combining like `ls -ll`, where there are multiple flags after a single dash. Each flag must be separate. The Go flag package also does not differentiate between long options and short ones. Finally, `-flag` and `--flag` are equivalent.

How to do it...

1. Open the console and create the folder `chapter01/recipe03`.
2. Navigate to the directory.
3. Create the `main.go` file with the following content:

```go
package main
import (
  "flag"
  "fmt"
  "log"
  "os"
  "strings"
)

// Custom type need to implement
// flag.Value interface to be able to
// use it in flag.Var function.
```

```go
type ArrayValue []string

func (s *ArrayValue) String() string {
  return fmt.Sprintf("%v", *s)
}

func (a *ArrayValue) Set(s string) error {
  *a = strings.Split(s, ",")
  return nil
}

func main() {

  // Extracting flag values with methods returning pointers
  retry := flag.Int("retry", -1, "Defines max retry count")

  // Read the flag using the XXXVar function.
  // In this case the variable must be defined
  // prior to the flag.
  var logPrefix string
  flag.StringVar(&logPrefix, "prefix", "", "Logger prefix")

  var arr ArrayValue
  flag.Var(&arr, "array", "Input array to iterate through.")

  // Execute the flag.Parse function, to
  // read the flags to defined variables.
  // Without this call the flag
  // variables remain empty.
  flag.Parse()

  // Sample logic not related to flags
  logger := log.New(os.Stdout, logPrefix, log.Ldate)

  retryCount := 0
  for retryCount < *retry {
    logger.Println("Retrying connection")
    logger.Printf("Sending array %v\n", arr)
    retryCount++
  }
}
```

4. Build the binary by executing the `go build -o util`.
5. From the console, execute `./util -retry 2 -prefix=example -array=1,2`.

6. See the output in the Terminal:

```
PROBLEMS    OUTPUT    DEBUG CONSOLE    TERMINAL    1: bash    ⇕    +    🗑    ∧    ✕
Macbooks-MacBook-Pro:recipe03 radek$ ./util -retry 2 -prefix=example -array=1,2
example2017/11/14 Retrying connection
example2017/11/14 Sending array [1 2]
example2017/11/14 Retrying connection
example2017/11/14 Sending array [1 2]
Macbooks-MacBook-Pro:recipe03 radek$ ▌
```

How it works...

For the flag definition in code, the `flag` package defines two types of functions.

The first type is the simple name of the flag type such as `Int`. This function will return the pointer to the integer variable where the value of the parsed flag is.

The `XXXVar` functions are the second type. These provide the same functionality, but you need to provide the pointer to the variable. The parsed flag value will be stored in the given variable.

The Go library also supports a custom flag type. The custom type must implement the `Value` interface from the `flag` package.

As an example, let's say the flag `retry` defines the retry limit for reconnecting to the endpoint, the `prefix` flag defines the prefix of each row in a log, and the `array` is the array flag that will be send as an payload to server. The program call from the Terminal will look like `./util -retry 2 -prefix=example array=1,2`.

The important part of the preceding code is the `Parse()` function which parses the defined flags from `Args[1:]`. The function must be called after all flags are defined and before the values are accessed.

The preceding code shows how to parse some data types from the command-line flags. Analogously, the other built-in types are parsed.

The last flag, `array`, demonstrates the definition of the custom type flag. Note that the `ArrayType` implements the `Value` interface from the `flag` package.

There's more…

The `flag` package contains more functions to design the interface with flags. It is worth reading the documentation for `FlagSet`.

By defining the new `FlagSet`, the arguments could be parsed by calling the `myFlagset.Parse(os.Args[2:])`. This way you can have flag subsets based on, for example, the first flag.

Getting and setting environment variables with default values

The previous recipe, *Creating a program interface with the flag package,* describes how to use flags as program parameters.

The other typical way of parameterization, especially for larger applications, is the configuration with the use of environment variables. Environment variables as a configuration option significantly simplify the deployment of the applications. These are also very common in cloud infrastructure.

Usually, the configuration of a database connection for a local and for an automated build environment is different.

If the configuration is defined by the environment variables, it is not necessary to change the application config files or even the application code. The exported environment variables (for example, `DBSTRING`) are all we need. It is also very practical to default the configuration if the environmental variable is not in place. This way, the life of the application developers is much easier.

This recipe will demonstrate how to read, set and unset the environment variable. It will also show you how to implement the default option if the variable is not set.

How to do it…

1. Open the console and create the folder `chapter01/recipe04`.
2. Navigate to the directory.

3. Create the `get.go` file with the following content:

```
package main

import (
  "log"
  "os"
)

func main() {
    connStr := os.Getenv("DB_CONN")
    log.Printf("Connection string: %s\n", connStr)
}
```

4. Execute the code by calling `DB_CONN=db:/user@example && go run get.go` in the Terminal.

5. See the output in the Terminal:

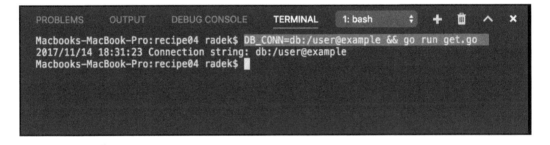

6. Create the `lookup.go` file with the following content:

```
package main

import (
  "log"
  "os"
)

func main() {

  key := "DB_CONN"
  connStr, ex := os.LookupEnv(key)
  if !ex {
    log.Printf("The env variable %s is not set.\n", key)
  }
  fmt.Println(connStr)
}
```

7. Execute the code by calling `unset DB_CONN && go run lookup.go` in the Terminal.

8. See the output in the Terminal:

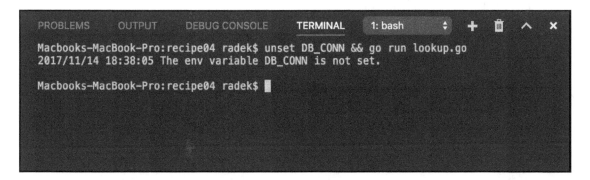

9. Create the `main.go` file with the following content:

```
package main
import (
  "log"
  "os"
)

func main() {

  key := "DB_CONN"
  // Set the environmental variable.
  os.Setenv(key, "postgres://as:as@example.com/pg?
                    sslmode=verify-full")
  val := GetEnvDefault(key, "postgres://as:as@localhost/pg?
                              sslmode=verify-full")
  log.Println("The value is :" + val)

  os.Unsetenv(key)
  val = GetEnvDefault(key, "postgres://as:as@127.0.0.1/pg?
                            sslmode=verify-full")
  log.Println("The default value is :" + val)

}

func GetEnvDefault(key, defVal string) string {
  val, ex := os.LookupEnv(key)
  if !ex {
    return defVal
  }
```

```
    return val
}
```

10. Run the code by executing `go run main.go`.
11. See the output in the Terminal:

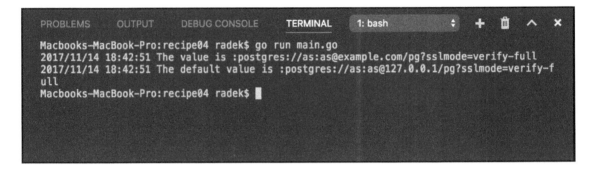

How it works...

The environment variables are accessed by the `Getenv` and `Setenv` functions in the `os` package. The names of the functions are self-explanatory and do not need any further description.

There is one more useful function in the `os` package. The `LookupEnv` function provides two values as a result; the value of the variable, and the boolean value which defines if the variable was set or not in the environment.

The disadvantage of the `os.Getenv` function is that it returns an empty string, even in cases where the environment variable is not set.

This handicap could be overcome by the `os.LookupEnv` function, which returns the string as a value of the environment variable and the boolean value that indicates whether the variable was set or not.

To implement the retrieval of the environment variable or the default one, use the `os.LookupEnv` function. Simply, if the variable is not set, which means that the second returned value is `false`, then the default value is returned. The use of the function is part of step 9.

Retrieving the current working directory

Another useful source of information for the application is the directory, where the program binary is located. With this information, the program can access the assets and files collocated with the binary file.

 This recipe is using the solution for Go since version 1.8. This one is the preferred one.

How to do it...

1. Open the console and create the folder chapter01/recipe05.
2. Navigate to the directory.
3. Create the main.go file with the following content:

```go
package main

import (
  "fmt"
  "os"
  "path/filepath"
)

func main() {
  ex, err := os.Executable()
  if err != nil {
    panic(err)
  }

  // Path to executable file
  fmt.Println(ex)

  // Resolve the direcotry
  // of the executable
  exPath := filepath.Dir(ex)
  fmt.Println("Executable path :" + exPath)

  // Use EvalSymlinks to get
  // the real path.
  realPath, err := filepath.EvalSymlinks(exPath)
  if err != nil {
```

```
        panic(err)
    }
    fmt.Println("Symlink evaluated:" + realPath)
}
```

4. Build the binary by the command `go build -o binary`.
5. Execute the binary by the Terminal call `./binary`.
6. See the output. It should display the absolute path on your machine:

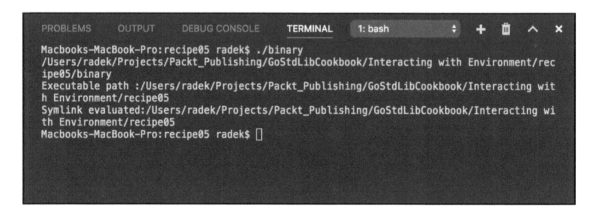

How it works...

Since Go 1.8, the `Executable` function from the `os` package is the preferred way of resolving the path of the executable. The `Executable` function returns the absolute path of the binary that is executed (unless the error is returned).

To resolve the directory from the binary path, the `Dir` from the `filepath` package is applied. The only pitfall of this is that the result could be the `symlink` or the path it pointed to.

To overcome this unstable behavior, the `EvalSymlinks` from the `filepath` package could be applied to the resultant path. With this hack, the returned value would be the real path of the binary.

The information about the directory where the binary is located could be obtained with the use of the `Executable` function in the `os` library.

Note that if the code is run by the command `go run`, the actual executable is located in a temporary directory.

Getting the current process PID

Getting to know the PID of the running process is useful. The PID could be used by OS utilities to find out the information about the process itself. It is also valuable to know the PID in case of process failure, so you can trace the process behavior across the system in system logs, such as /var/log/messages, /var/log/syslog.

This recipe shows you how to use the os package to obtain a PID of the executed program, and use it with the operating system utility to obtain some more information.

How to do it...

1. Open the console and create the folder chapter01/recipe06.
2. Navigate to the directory.
3. Create the main.go file with the following content:

```go
package main

import (
  "fmt"
  "os"
  "os/exec"
  "strconv"
)

func main() {

  pid := os.Getpid()
  fmt.Printf("Process PID: %d \n", pid)

  prc := exec.Command("ps", "-p", strconv.Itoa(pid), "-v")
  out, err := prc.Output()
  if err != nil {
    panic(err)
  }

  fmt.Println(string(out))
}
```

4. Run the code by executing the go run main.go.

5. See the output in the Terminal:

```
PROBLEMS    OUTPUT    DEBUG CONSOLE    TERMINAL    1: bash              +  🗑  ∧  ✕
Macbooks-MacBook-Pro:recipe06 radek$ go run main.go
Process PID: 23592
  PID STAT      TIME  SL  RE PAGEIN       VSZ    RSS  LIM     TSIZ %CPU %MEM COMMAND
23592 S+     0:00.01   0   0      0 556598592   1408    -        0  0.0  0.0 /var/fold
ers/wf/v0krj6_x2tb9gsdmvx2msbg40000gp/T/go-build809876414/command-line-arguments/_obj/ex
e/main

Macbooks-MacBook-Pro:recipe06 radek$ █
```

How it works...

The function `Getpid` from the `os` package returns the PID of a process. The sample code shows how to get more information on the process from the operating system utility `ps`.

It could be useful to print the PID at the start of the application, so at the time of the crash, the cause could also be investigated by the retrieved PID.

Handling operating system signals

Signals are the elementary way the operating systems communicate with the running process. Two of the most usual signals are called `SIGINT` and `SIGTERM`. These cause the program to terminate.

There are also signals such as `SIGHUP`. `SIGHUP` indicates that the terminal which called the process was closed and, for example, the program could decide to move to the background.

Go provides a way of handling the behavior in case the application received the signal. This recipe will provide an example of implementing the handling.

How to do it...

1. Open the console and create the folder `chapter01/recipe07`.
2. Navigate to the directory.
3. Create the `main.go` file with the following content:

```go
package main

import (
    "fmt"
    "os"
    "os/signal"
    "syscall"
)

func main() {

    // Create the channel where the received
    // signal would be sent. The Notify
    // will not block when the signal
    // is sent and the channel is not ready.
    // So it is better to
    // create buffered channel.
    sChan := make(chan os.Signal, 1)

    // Notify will catch the
    // given signals and send
    // the os.Signal value
    // through the sChan.
    // If no signal specified in
    // argument, all signals are matched.
    signal.Notify(sChan,
        syscall.SIGHUP,
        syscall.SIGINT,
        syscall.SIGTERM,
        syscall.SIGQUIT)

    // Create channel to wait till the
    // signal is handled.
    exitChan := make(chan int)
    go func() {
        signal := <-sChan
        switch signal {
            case syscall.SIGHUP:
                fmt.Println("The calling terminal has been closed")
                exitChan <- 0
```

```
        case syscall.SIGINT:
          fmt.Println("The process has been interrupted by CTRL+C")
          exitChan <- 1

        case syscall.SIGTERM:
          fmt.Println("kill SIGTERM was executed for process")
          exitChan <- 1

        case syscall.SIGQUIT:
          fmt.Println("kill SIGQUIT was executed for process")
          exitChan <- 1
      }
    }()

    code := <-exitChan
    os.Exit(code)
}
```

4. Run the code by executing `go run main.go`.
5. Send the `SIGINT` signal to the application by pressing *CTRL + C*.
6. See the output:

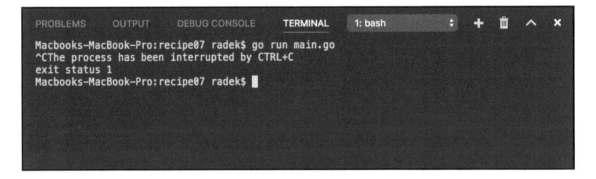

How it works...

In an application, where the resources are acquired, a resource leak could happen in the case of an instant termination. It is better to handle the signals and take some necessary steps to release the resources. The preceding code shows the concept of how to do that.

The `Notify` function from the `signal` package would be the one that helps us to handle the received signals.

If no signal is specified as an argument in a `Notify` function, the function will catch all possible signals.

Note that the `Notify` function of the `signal` package is communicating with the `goroutine` by the `sChan` channel. `Notify` then catches the defined signals and sends these to `goroutine` to be handled. Finally, `exitChan` is used to resolve the exit code of the process.

The important information is that the `Notify` function will not block the signal if the assigned channel is not ready. This way the signal could be missed. To avoid missing the signal, it is better to create the buffered channel.

Note that the `SIGKILL` and `SIGSTOP` signals may not be caught by the `Notify` function, thus it is not possible to handle these.

Calling an external process

The Go binary could also be used as a tool for various utilities and with use of `go run` as a replacement for the bash script. For these purposes, it is usual that the command-line utilities are called.

In this recipe, the basics of how to execute and handle the child process will be provided.

Getting ready

Test if the following commands work in your Terminal:

1. Test if the `ls` (`dir` for Windows) command exists in your `$PATH`.
2. You should be able to execute the `ls` (`dir` in Windows) command in your Terminal.

How to do it...

The following steps cover the solution:

1. Open the console and create the folder `chapter01/recipe08`.
2. Navigate to the directory.
3. Create the `run.go` file with the following content:

```go
package main

import (
  "bytes"
  "fmt"
  "os/exec"
)

func main() {

  prc := exec.Command("ls", "-a")
  out := bytes.NewBuffer([]byte{})
  prc.Stdout = out
  err := prc.Run()
  if err != nil {
    fmt.Println(err)
  }

  if prc.ProcessState.Success() {
    fmt.Println("Process run successfully with output:\n")
    fmt.Println(out.String())
  }
}
```

4. Run the code by executing `go run run.go`.

5. See the output in the Terminal:

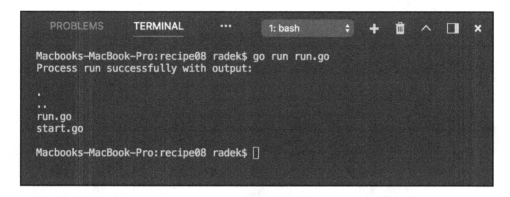

6. Create the `start.go` file with the following content:

```go
package main

import (
    "fmt"
    "os/exec"
)

func main() {

    prc := exec.Command("ls", "-a")
    err := prc.Start()
    if err != nil {
        fmt.Println(err)
    }

    prc.Wait()

    if prc.ProcessState.Success() {
        fmt.Println("Process run successfully with output:\n")
        fmt.Println(out.String())
    }
}
```

7. Run the code by executing `go run start.go`.

8. See the output in Terminal:

How it works...

The Go standard library provides a simple way of calling the external process. This could be done by the `Command` function of the `os/exec` package.

The simplest way is to create the `Cmd` struct and call the `Run` function. The `Run` function executes the process and waits until it completes. If the command exited with an error, the `err` value is not null.

This is more suitable for calling the OS utils and tools, so the program does not hang too long.

The process could be executed asynchronously too. This is done by calling the `Start` method of the `Cmd` structure. In this case, the process is executed, but the main `goroutine` does not wait until it ends. The `Wait` method could be used to wait until the process ends. After the `Wait` method finishes, the resources of the process are released.

This approach is more suitable for executing long-running processes and services that the program depends on.

See also

This recipe describes how to simply execute the child process. There are *Retrieve child process information* and *Reading/writing from the child process* recipes in this chapter that also provide the steps on how to read from and write to the child process, and get useful information about the process.

Retrieving child process information

The recipe *Calling an external process* describes how to call the child process, synchronously and asynchronously. Naturally, to handle the process behavior you need to find out more about the process. This recipe shows how to obtain the PID and elementary information about the child process after it terminates.

The information about the running process could be obtained only via the `syscall` package and it is highly platform-dependent.

Getting ready

Test if the `sleep` (`timeout` for Windows) command exists in the Terminal.

How to do it...

1. Open the console and create the folder `chapter01/recipe09`.
2. Navigate to the directory.
3. Create the `main_running.go` file with the following content:

```
package main

import (
  "fmt"
  "os/exec"
  "runtime"
)

func main() {

  var cmd string
  if runtime.GOOS == "windows" {
```

```
      cmd = "timeout"
    } else {
      cmd = "sleep"
    }
    proc := exec.Command(cmd, "1")
    proc.Start()

    // No process state is returned
    // till the process finish.
    fmt.Printf("Process state for running process: %v\n",
              proc.ProcessState)

    // The PID could be obtain
    // event for the running process
    fmt.Printf("PID of running process: %d\n\n",
              proc.Process.Pid)
  }
```

4. Run the code by executing `go run main_running.go`.

5. See the output in the Terminal:

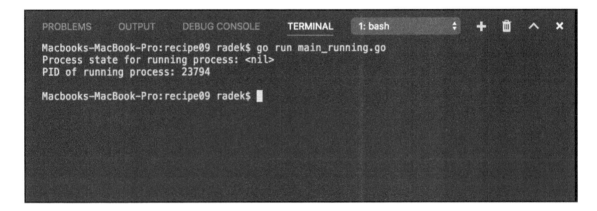

6. Create the `main.go` file with the following content:

```
func main() {

  var cmd string
  if runtime.GOOS == "windows" {
    cmd = "timeout"
  } else {
    cmd = "sleep"
  }
```

```
        proc := exec.Command(cmd, "1")
        proc.Start()

        // Wait function will
        // wait till the process ends.
        proc.Wait()

        // After the process terminates
        // the *os.ProcessState contains
        // simple information
        // about the process run
        fmt.Printf("PID: %d\n", proc.ProcessState.Pid())
        fmt.Printf("Process took: %dms\n",
                proc.ProcessState.SystemTime()/time.Microsecond)
        fmt.Printf("Exited sucessfuly : %t\n",
                proc.ProcessState.Success())
}
```

7. Run the code by executing `go run main.go`.
8. See the output in the Terminal:

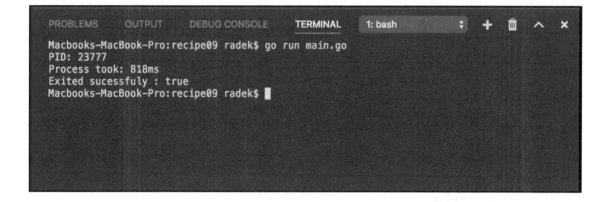

How it works...

The os/exec standard library provides the way to execute the process.
Using Command, the Cmd structure is returned. The Cmd provides the access to process the representation. When the process is running, you can only find out the PID.

There is only a little information that you can retrieve about the process. But by retrieving the PID of the process, you are able to call the utilities from the OS to get more information.

 Remember that it is possible to obtain the PID of the child process, even if it is running. On the other hand, the ProcessState structure of the os package is available, only after the process terminates.

See also

There are *Reading/writing from the child process* and *Calling an external process* recipes in this chapter that are related to process handling.

Reading/writing from the child process

Every process, that is executed, has the standard output, input and error output. The Go standard library provides the way to read and write to these.

This recipe will walk through the approaches on how to read the output and write to the input of the child process.

Getting ready

Verify if the following commands work in the Terminal:

1. Test if the ls (dir for Windows) command exists in the Terminal.
2. You should be able to execute the ls (dir in Windows) command in your Terminal.

How to do it...

1. Open the console and create the folder `chapter01/recipe10`.
2. Navigate to the directory.
3. Create the `main_read_output.go` file with the following content:

```go
package main

import (
  "fmt"
  "os/exec"
  "runtime"
)

func main() {

  var cmd string

  if runtime.GOOS == "windows" {
    cmd = "dir"
  } else {
    cmd = "ls"
  }

  proc := exec.Command(cmd)

  // Output will run the process
  // terminates and returns the standard
  // output in a byte slice.
  buff, err := proc.Output()

  if err != nil {
    panic(err)
  }

  // The output of child
  // process in form
  // of byte slice
  // printed as string
  fmt.Println(string(buff))

}
```

4. Run the code by executing `go run main_read_output.go`.

5. See the output in the Terminal:

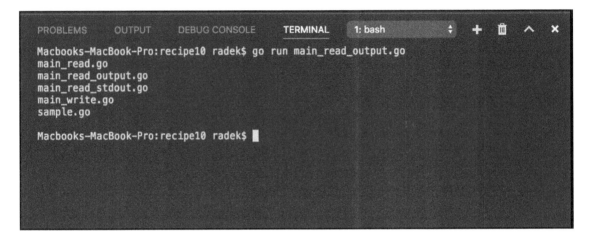

6. Create the `main_read_stdout.go` file with the following content:

```
package main

import (
  "bytes"
  "fmt"
  "os/exec"
  "runtime"
)

func main() {

  var cmd string

  if runtime.GOOS == "windows" {
    cmd = "dir"
  } else {
    cmd = "ls"
  }

  proc := exec.Command(cmd)

  buf := bytes.NewBuffer([]byte{})

  // The buffer which implements
  // io.Writer interface is assigned to
```

```
// Stdout of the process
proc.Stdout = buf

// To avoid race conditions
// in this example. We wait till
// the process exit.
proc.Run()

// The process writes the output to
// to buffer and we use the bytes
// to print the output.
fmt.Println(string(buf.Bytes()))

}
```

7. Run the code by executing `go run main_read_stdout.go`.
8. See the output in the Terminal:

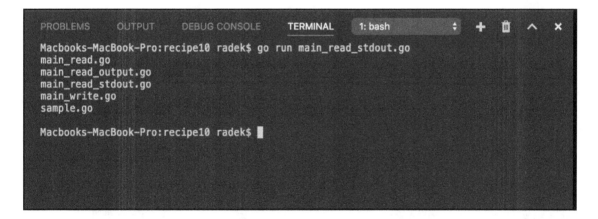

9. Create the `main_read_read.go` file with the following content:

```
package main

import (
    "bufio"
    "context"
    "fmt"
    "os/exec"
    "time"
)

func main() {
```

```
        cmd := "ping"
        timeout := 2 * time.Second

        // The command line tool
        // "ping" is executed for
        // 2 seconds
        ctx, _ := context.WithTimeout(context.TODO(), timeout)
        proc := exec.CommandContext(ctx, cmd, "example.com")

        // The process output is obtained
        // in form of io.ReadCloser. The underlying
        // implementation use the os.Pipe
        stdout, _ := proc.StdoutPipe()
        defer stdout.Close()

        // Start the process
        proc.Start()

        // For more comfortable reading the
        // bufio.Scanner is used.
        // The read call is blocking.
        s := bufio.NewScanner(stdout)
        for s.Scan() {
          fmt.Println(s.Text())
        }
    }
```

10. Run the code by executing `go run main_read.go`.

11. See the output in the Terminal:

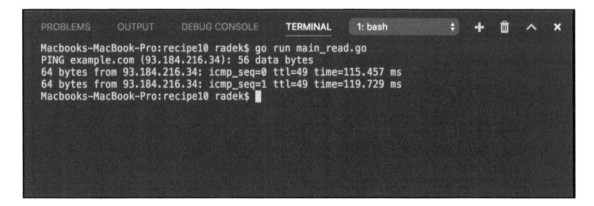

12. Create the `sample.go` file with the following content:

```go
package main

import (
  "bufio"
  "fmt"
  "os"
)

func main() {
  sc := bufio.NewScanner(os.Stdin)

  for sc.Scan() {
    fmt.Println(sc.Text())
  }
}
```

13. Create the `main.go` file with the following content:

```go
package main

import (
  "bufio"
  "fmt"
  "io"
  "os/exec"
  "time"
)

func main() {
  cmd := []string{"go", "run", "sample.go"}

  // The command line tool
  // "ping" is executed for
  // 2 seconds
  proc := exec.Command(cmd[0], cmd[1], cmd[2])

  // The process input is obtained
  // in form of io.WriteCloser. The underlying
  // implementation use the os.Pipe
  stdin, _ := proc.StdinPipe()
  defer stdin.Close()

  // For debugging purposes we watch the
  // output of the executed process
  stdout, _ := proc.StdoutPipe()
```

```
defer stdout.Close()

go func() {
  s := bufio.NewScanner(stdout)
  for s.Scan() {
    fmt.Println("Program says:" + s.Text())
  }
}()

// Start the process
proc.Start()

// Now the following lines
// are written to child
// process standard input
fmt.Println("Writing input")
io.WriteString(stdin, "Hello\n")
io.WriteString(stdin, "Golang\n")
io.WriteString(stdin, "is awesome\n")

time.Sleep(time.Second * 2)

proc.Process.Kill()

}
```

14. Run the code by executing `go run main.go`.

15. See the output in the Terminal:

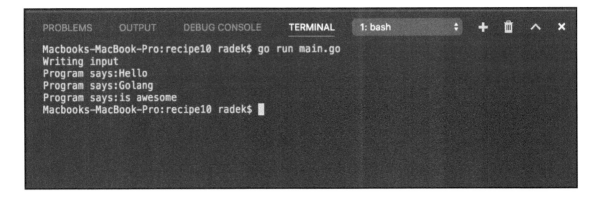

How it works...

The Cmd structure of the os/exec package provides the functions to access the output/input of the process. There are a few approaches to read the output of the process.

One of the simplest ways to read the process output is to use the Output or CombinedOutput method of the Cmd structure (gets Stderr and Stdout). While calling this function, the program synchronously waits till the child process terminates and then returns the output to a byte buffer.

Besides the Output and OutputCombined methods, the Cmd structure provides the Stdout property, where the io.Writer could be assigned. The assigned writer then serves as a destination for the process output. It could be a file, byte buffer or any type implementing the io.Writer interface.

The last approach to read the process output is to get the io.Reader from the Cmd structure by calling the StdoutPipe method. The StdoutPipe method creates the pipe between the Stdout, where the process writes the output, and provides Reader which works as the interface for the program to read the process output. This way the output of the process is piped to the retrieved io.Reader .

Writing to a process stdin works the same way. Of all the options, the one with io.Writer will be demonstrated.

As could be seen, there are a few ways to read and write from the child process. The use of stderr and stdin is almost the same as described in steps 6-7. Finally, the approach of how to access the input/output could be divided this way:

- Synchronous (wait until the process ends and get the bytes): The Output and CombinedOutput methods of Cmd are used.
- IO: The output or input are provided in the form of io.Writer/Reader. The XXXPipe and StdXXX properties are the right ones for this approach.

The IO type is more flexible and could also be used asynchronously.

Shutting down the application gracefully

Servers and daemons are the programs that run for a long time (typically days or even weeks). These long-running programs usually allocate resources (database connections, network sock) at the start and keep these resources as long as they exist. If such a process is killed and the shutdown is not handled properly, a resource leak could happen. To avoid that behavior, the so-called graceful shutdown should be implemented.

Graceful, in this case, means that the application catches the termination signal, if possible, and tries to clean up and release the allocated resources before it terminates. This recipe will show you how to implement the graceful shutdown.

The recipe, *Handling operating system signals* describes the catching of OS signals. The same approach will be used for implementing the graceful shutdown. Before the program terminates, it will clean up and carry out some other activities.

How to do it...

1. Open the console and create the folder `chapter01/recipe11`.
2. Navigate to the directory.
3. Create the `main.go` file with the following content:

```go
package main

import (
  "fmt"
  "io"
  "log"
  "os"
  "os/signal"
  "syscall"
  "time"
)

var writer *os.File

func main() {

  // The file is opened as
  // a log file to write into.
  // This way we represent the resources
  // allocation.
```

```go
var err error
writer, err = os.OpenFile(fmt.Sprintf("test_%d.log",
        time.Now().Unix()), os.O_RDWR|os.O_CREATE, os.ModePerm)
if err != nil {
  panic(err)
}

// The code is running in a goroutine
// independently. So in case the program is
// terminated from outside, we need to
// let the goroutine know via the closeChan
closeChan := make(chan bool)
go func() {
  for {
    time.Sleep(time.Second)
    select {
      case <-closeChan:
        log.Println("Goroutine closing")
        return
      default:
        log.Println("Writing to log")
        io.WriteString(writer, fmt.Sprintf("Logging access
                    %s\n", time.Now().String()))
    }

  }
}()

sigChan := make(chan os.Signal, 1)
signal.Notify(sigChan,
  syscall.SIGTERM,
  syscall.SIGQUIT,
  syscall.SIGINT)

// This is blocking read from
// sigChan where the Notify function sends
// the signal.
<-sigChan

// After the signal is received
// all the code behind the read from channel could be
// considered as a cleanup.
// CLEANUP SECTION
close(closeChan)
releaseAllResources()
fmt.Println("The application shut down gracefully")
}
```

```
func releaseAllResources() {
  io.WriteString(writer, "Application releasing
                all resources\n")
  writer.Close()
}
```

4. Run the code by executing `go run main.go`.

5. Press *CTRL + C* to send a `SIGINT` signal.

6. Wait until the Terminal output looks like this:

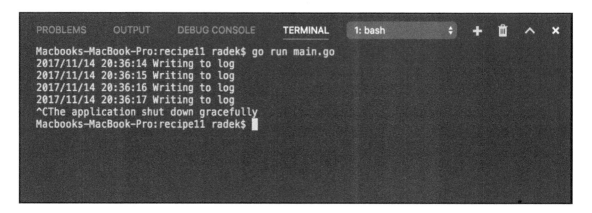

7. The `recipe11` folder should also contain a file called `test_XXXX.log`, which contains lines like this:

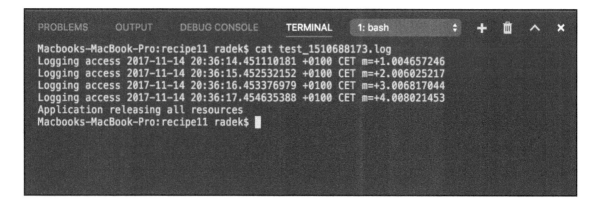

How it works...

The reading from a `sigChan` is blocking so the program keeps running until the Signal is sent through the channel. The `sigChan` is the channel where the `Notify` function sends the signals.

The main code of the program runs in a new `goroutine`. This way, the work continues while the main function is blocked on the `sigChan`. Once the signal from operation system is sent to process, the `sigChan` receives the signal and the code below the line where the reading from the `sigChan` channel is executed. This code section could be considered as the cleanup section.

Note that the step 7 terminal output contains the final log, `Application releasing all resources`, which is part of the cleanup section.

See also

A detailed description of how the signal catching works is in the recipe *Handling operating system signals*.

File configuration with functional options

This recipe is not directly related to the Go standard library but includes how to handle an optional configuration for your application. The recipe will use the functional options pattern in a real case with a file configuration.

How to do it...

1. Open the console and create the folder `chapter01/recipe12`.
2. Navigate to the directory.
3. Create the `main.go` file with the following content:

```
package main

import (
  "encoding/json"
  "fmt"
  "os"
```

```
)

type Client struct {
  consulIP string
  connString string
}

func (c *Client) String() string {
  return fmt.Sprintf("ConsulIP: %s , Connection String: %s",
                     c.consulIP, c.connString)
}

var defaultClient = Client{
  consulIP: "localhost:9000",
  connString: "postgres://localhost:5432",
}

// ConfigFunc works as a type to be used
// in functional options
type ConfigFunc func(opt *Client)

// FromFile func returns the ConfigFunc
// type. So this way it could read the configuration
// from the json.
func FromFile(path string) ConfigFunc {
  return func(opt *Client) {
    f, err := os.Open(path)
    if err != nil {
      panic(err)
    }
    defer f.Close()
    decoder := json.NewDecoder(f)

    fop := struct {
      ConsulIP string `json:"consul_ip"`
    }{}
    err = decoder.Decode(&fop)
    if err != nil {
      panic(err)
    }
    opt.consulIP = fop.ConsulIP
  }
}

// FromEnv reads the configuration
// from the environmental variables
// and combines them with existing ones.
func FromEnv() ConfigFunc {
```

```
      return func(opt *Client) {
        connStr, exist := os.LookupEnv("CONN_DB")
        if exist {
          opt.connString = connStr
        }
      }
    }

    func NewClient(opts ...ConfigFunc) *Client {
      client := defaultClient
      for _, val := range opts {
        val(&client)
      }
      return &client
    }

    func main() {
      client := NewClient(FromFile("config.json"), FromEnv())
      fmt.Println(client.String())
    }
```

4. In the same folder, create the file `config.json` with content:

```
    {
      "consul_ip":"127.0.0.1"
    }
```

5. Execute the code by the command `CONN_DB=oracle://local:5921 go run main.go`.

6. See the output:

How it works...

The core concept of the functional options pattern is that the configuration API contains the functional parameters. In this case, the NewClient function accepts a various number of ConfigFunc arguments, which are then applied one by one on the defaultClient struct. This way, the default configuration is modified with huge flexibility.

See the FromFile and FromEnv functions, which return the ConfigFunc, that is in fact, accessing the file or environmental variables.

Finally, you can check the output which applied both the configuration options and resulting Client struct that contains the values from the file and environmental variables.

2
Strings and Things

The recipes in this chapter are:

- Finding the substring in a string
- Breaking the string into words
- Joining the string slice with a separator
- Concatenating a string with writer
- Aligning text with tabwriter
- Replacing part of the string
- Finding the substring in text by the regex pattern
- Decoding a string from the non-Unicode charset
- Controlling case
- Parsing comma-separated data
- Managing whitespace in a string
- Indenting a text document

Introduction

Operations on strings and string-based data are common tasks in a developer's life. This chapter covers how to handle these using the Go standard library. It is no surprise that with the standard library it is possible to do a great deal.

 Check whether Go is properly installed. The *Getting ready* section from the *Retrieving the Golang version* recipe of `Chapter 1`, *Interacting with the Environment,* will help you.

Finding the substring in a string

Finding the substring in a string is one of the most common tasks for developers. Most of the mainstream languages implement this in a standard library. Go is not an exception. This recipe describes the way Go implements this.

How to do it...

1. Open the console and create the folder `chapter02/recipe01`.
2. Navigate to the directory.
3. Create the `contains.go` file with the following content:

```
package main

import (
  "fmt"
  "strings"
)

const refString = "Mary had a little lamb"

func main() {

  lookFor := "lamb"
  contain := strings.Contains(refString, lookFor)
  fmt.Printf("The \"%s\" contains \"%s\": %t \n", refString,
          lookFor, contain)

  lookFor = "wolf"
  contain = strings.Contains(refString, lookFor)
  fmt.Printf("The \"%s\" contains \"%s\": %t \n", refString,
          lookFor, contain)

  startsWith := "Mary"
  starts := strings.HasPrefix(refString, startsWith)
  fmt.Printf("The \"%s\" starts with \"%s\": %t \n", refString,
          startsWith, starts)

  endWith := "lamb"
  ends := strings.HasSuffix(refString, endWith)
  fmt.Printf("The \"%s\" ends with \"%s\": %t \n", refString,
          endWith, ends)
```

}

4. Run the code by executing `go run contains.go`.

5. See the output in the Terminal:

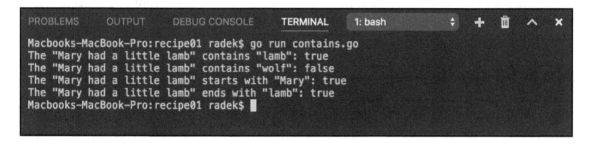

```
PROBLEMS      OUTPUT      DEBUG CONSOLE      TERMINAL      1: bash
Macbooks-MacBook-Pro:recipe01 radek$ go run contains.go
The "Mary had a little lamb" contains "lamb": true
The "Mary had a little lamb" contains "wolf": false
The "Mary had a little lamb" starts with "Mary": true
The "Mary had a little lamb" ends with "lamb": true
Macbooks-MacBook-Pro:recipe01 radek$
```

How it works...

The Go library `strings` contain functions to handle the string operations. This time the function `Contains` could be used. The `Contains` function simply checks whether the string has a given substring. In fact, the function `Index` is used in `Contains` function.

To check whether the string begins with the substring, the `HasPrefix` function is there. To check whether the string ends with the substring, the function `HasSuffix` will work.

In fact, the `Contains` function is implemented by use of the `Index` function from the same package. As you can guess, the actual implementation works like this: if the index of the given substring is greater than -1, the `Contains` function returns `true`.

The `HasPrefix` and `HasSuffix` functions work in a different way: the internal implementation just checks the length of both the string and substring, and if they are equal or the string is longer, the required part of the string is compared.

See also

This recipe describes how to match the exact substring. The *Finding the substring in text by the regex pattern* recipe will help to find out how to use regex pattern matching.

Breaking the string into words

Breaking the string into words could be tricky. First, decide what the word is, as well as what the separator is, and if there is any whitespace or any other characters. After these decisions have been made, you can choose the appropriate function from the strings package. This recipe will describe common cases.

How to do it...

1. Open the console and create the folder chapter02/recipe02.
2. Navigate to the directory.
3. Create the whitespace.go file with the following content:

```go
package main

import (
  "fmt"
  "strings"
)

const refString = "Mary had a little lamb"

func main() {

  words := strings.Fields(refString)
  for idx, word := range words {
    fmt.Printf("Word %d is: %s\n", idx, word)
  }

}
```

4. Run the code by executing `go run whitespace.go`.

5. See the output in the Terminal:

```
PROBLEMS    OUTPUT    DEBUG CONSOLE    TERMINAL    1: bash    +  🗑  ∧  ✕
Macbooks-MacBook-Pro:recipe02 radek$ go run whitespace.go
Word 0 is: Mary
Word 1 is: had
Word 2 is: a
Word 3 is: little
Word 4 is: lamb
Macbooks-MacBook-Pro:recipe02 radek$ ▮
```

6. Create another file called `anyother.go` with the following content:

```go
package main

import (
  "fmt"
  "strings"
)

const refString = "Mary_had a little_lamb"

func main() {

  words := strings.Split(refString, "_")
  for idx, word := range words {
    fmt.Printf("Word %d is: %s\n", idx, word)
  }

}
```

7. Run the code by executing `go run anyother.go`.

8. See the output in the Terminal:

```
PROBLEMS    OUTPUT    DEBUG CONSOLE    TERMINAL    1: bash    +  🗑  ∧  ✕
Macbooks-MacBook-Pro:recipe02 radek$ go run anyother.go
Word 0 is: Mary
Word 1 is: had a little
Word 2 is: lamb
Macbooks-MacBook-Pro:recipe02 radek$ ▮
```

9. Create another file called `specfunction.go` with the following content:

```go
package main

import (
  "fmt"
  "strings"
)

const refString = "Mary*had,a%little_lamb"

func main() {

  // The splitFunc is called for each
  // rune in a string. If the rune
  // equals any of character in a "*%,_"
  // the refString is split.
  splitFunc := func(r rune) bool {
    return strings.ContainsRune("*%,_", r)
  }

  words := strings.FieldsFunc(refString, splitFunc)
  for idx, word := range words {
    fmt.Printf("Word %d is: %s\n", idx, word)
  }

}
```

10. Run the code by executing `go run specfunction.go`.

11. See the output in the Terminal:

```
PROBLEMS    OUTPUT    DEBUG CONSOLE    TERMINAL    1: bash
Macbooks-MacBook-Pro:recipe02 radek$ go run specfunction.go
Word 0 is: Mary
Word 1 is: had
Word 2 is: a
Word 3 is: little
Word 4 is: lamb
Macbooks-MacBook-Pro:recipe02 radek$
```

12. Create another file called `regex.go` with the following content:

```go
package main

import (
  "fmt"
  "regexp"
)

const refString = "Mary*had,a%little_lamb"

func main() {

  words := regexp.MustCompile("[*,%_]{1}").Split(refString, -1)
  for idx, word := range words {
    fmt.Printf("Word %d is: %s\n", idx, word)
  }

}
```

13. Run the code by executing `go run regex.go`.

14. See the output in the Terminal:

How it works...

The simplest form of how to split the string into words considers any whitespace as a separator. In detail, the whitespace is defined by the `IsSpace` function in the `unicode` package:

```
'\t', '\n', '\v', '\f', '\r', ' ', U+0085 (NEL), U+00A0 (NBSP).
```

The `Fields` function of the `strings` package could be used to split the sentence by the whitespace chars as mentioned earlier. The steps **1 – 5** cover this first simple case.

If any other separator is needed, the `Split` function comes into play. Splitting by another separator is covered in steps **6 – 8**. Just note that the whitespace in the string is omitted.

If you need a more complex function to decide whether to split the string at a given point, `FieldsFunc` could work for you. One of the function's argument is the function that consumes the rune of the given string and returns `true` if the string should split at that point. This option is covered by steps **9 – 11**.

The regular expression is the last option mentioned in the example. The `Regexp` structure of the `regexp` package contains the `Split` method, which works as you would expect. It splits the string in the place of the matching group. This approach is used in steps **12 – 14**.

There's more...

The `strings` package also provides the various `SplitXXX` functions that could help you to achieve more specific tasks.

Joining the string slice with a separator

The recipe, *Breaking the string into words*, led us through the task of splitting the single string into substrings, according to defined rules. This recipe, on the other hand, describes how to concatenate the multiple strings into a single string with a given string as the separator.

A real use case could be the problem of dynamically building a SQL select statement condition.

How to do it...

1. Open the console and create the folder `chapter02/recipe03`.
2. Navigate to the directory.
3. Create the `join.go` file with the following content:

```
package main

import (
  "fmt"
  "strings"
)
```

```
const selectBase = "SELECT * FROM user WHERE %s "

var refStringSlice = []string{
  " FIRST_NAME = 'Jack' ",
  " INSURANCE_NO = 333444555 ",
  " EFFECTIVE_FROM = SYSDATE "}

func main() {

  sentence := strings.Join(refStringSlice, "AND")
  fmt.Printf(selectBase+"\n", sentence)

}
```

4. Run the code by executing `go run join.go`.

5. See the output in the Terminal:

6. Create the `join_manually.go` file with the following content:

```
package main

import (
  "fmt"
  "strings"
)

const selectBase = "SELECT * FROM user WHERE "

var refStringSlice = []string{
  " FIRST_NAME = 'Jack' ",
  " INSURANCE_NO = 333444555 ",
  " EFFECTIVE_FROM = SYSDATE "}

type JoinFunc func(piece string) string

func main() {

  jF := func(p string) string {
```

```
        if strings.Contains(p, "INSURANCE") {
          return "OR"
        }

        return "AND"
    }
    result := JoinWithFunc(refStringSlice, jF)
    fmt.Println(selectBase + result)
}

func JoinWithFunc(refStringSlice []string,
                  joinFunc JoinFunc) string {
    concatenate := refStringSlice[0]
    for _, val := range refStringSlice[1:] {
      concatenate = concatenate + joinFunc(val) + val
    }
    return concatenate
}
```

7. Run the code by executing go run join.go.

8. See the output in the Terminal:

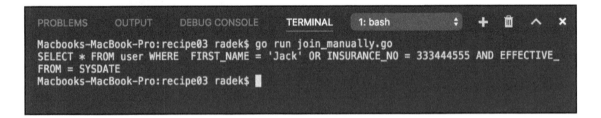

How it works...

For the purpose of joining the string slice into a single string, the Join function of the strings package is there. Simply, you need to provide the slice with strings that are needed to be joined. This way you can comfortably join the string slices. The use of the Join function is shown in steps **1 – 5**.

Naturally, the joining could be implemented manually by iterating over the slice. This way you can customize the separator by some more complex logic. The steps **6 – 8** just represent how the manual concatenation could be used with more complex decision logic, based on the string that is currently processed.

There's more...

The Join function is provided by the bytes package, which naturally serves to join the slice of bytes.

Concatenating a string with writer

Besides the built-in + operator, there are more ways to concatenate the string. This recipe will describe the more performant way of concatenating strings with the bytes package and the built-in copy function.

How to do it...

1. Open the console and create the folder chapter02/recipe04.
2. Navigate to the directory.
3. Create the concat_buffer.go file with the following content:

```
package main

import (
  "bytes"
  "fmt"
)

func main() {
  strings := []string{"This ", "is ", "even ",
                      "more ", "performant "}
  buffer := bytes.Buffer{}
  for _, val := range strings {
    buffer.WriteString(val)
  }

  fmt.Println(buffer.String())
}
```

4. Run the code by executing `go run concat_buffer.go`.

5. See the output in the Terminal:

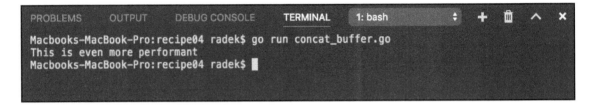

6. Create the `concat_copy.go` file with the following content:

```
package main

import (
  "fmt"
)

func main() {

    strings := []string{"This ", "is ", "even ",
                        "more ", "performant "}

    bs := make([]byte, 100)
    bl := 0

    for _, val := range strings {
      bl += copy(bs[bl:], []byte(val))
    }

    fmt.Println(string(bs[:]))

}
```

7. Run the code by executing `go run concat_copy.go`.

8. See the output in the Terminal:

How it works...

The steps **1 - 5** cover the use of the `bytes` package `Buffer` as a performance-friendly solution to string concatenation. The `Buffer` structure implements the `WriteString` method, which could be used to effectively concatenate the strings into an underlying byte slice.

There is no need to use this improvement in all situations, just think about this in cases where the program is going to concatenate a big number of strings (for example, in-memory CSV exports and others).

The built-in `copy` function presented in steps **6 - 8** could be used to accomplish the `string` concatenation. This method requires some assumption about the final string length, or it could be done on the fly. However, if the capacity of the buffer, where the result is written, is smaller than the sum of the already written part and the string to be appended, the buffer must be expanded (usually by the allocation of a new slice with bigger capacity).

There's more...

Just for comparison, there is a benchmark code, which compares the performance of the built-in + operator, `bytes.Buffer`, and built-in `copy`:

1. Create a `bench` folder and file `bench_test.go` in it with the following content:

```go
package main

import (
  "bytes"
  "testing"
)

const testString = "test"

func BenchmarkConcat(b *testing.B) {
  var str string
  b.ResetTimer()
  for n := 0; n < b.N; n++ {
    str += testString
  }
  b.StopTimer()
}

func BenchmarkBuffer(b *testing.B) {
```

```
var buffer bytes.Buffer

b.ResetTimer()
for n := 0; n < b.N; n++ {
  buffer.WriteString(testString)
}
b.StopTimer()
}

func BenchmarkCopy(b *testing.B) {
  bs := make([]byte, b.N)
  bl := 0

  b.ResetTimer()
  for n := 0; n < b.N; n++ {
    bl += copy(bs[bl:], testString)
  }
  b.StopTimer()
}
```

2. See the results of the benchmark run:

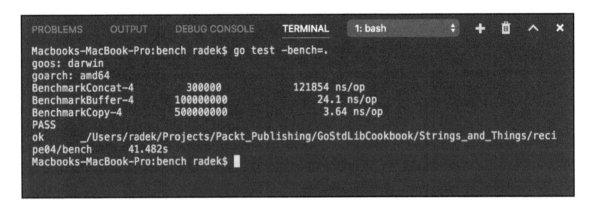

Aligning text with tabwriter

In certain cases, the output (usually data output) is done via tabbed text, which is formatted in well-arranged cells. This format could be achieved with the `text/tabwriter` package. The package provides the `Writer` filter, which transforms the text with the tab characters into properly formatted output text.

How to do it...

1. Open the console and create the folder `chapter02/recipe05`.
2. Navigate to the directory.
3. Create the `tabwriter.go` file with the following content:

```
package main

import (
  "fmt"
  "os"
  "text/tabwriter"
)

func main() {

    w := tabwriter.NewWriter(os.Stdout, 15, 0, 1, ' ',
                              tabwriter.AlignRight)
    fmt.Fprintln(w, "username\tfirstname\tlastname\t")
    fmt.Fprintln(w, "sohlich\tRadomir\tSohlich\t")
    fmt.Fprintln(w, "novak\tJohn\tSmith\t")
    w.Flush()

}
```

4. Run the code by executing `go run tabwriter.go`.
5. See the output in the Terminal:

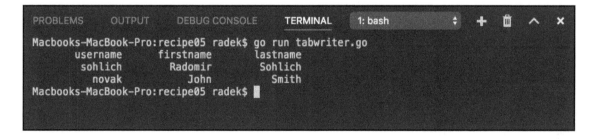

How it works...

The `NewWriter` function call creates the `Writer` filter with configured parameters. All data written by this `Writer` is formatted according to the parameters. `os.Stdout` is used here for demonstration purposes.

The `text/tabwriter` package also provides a few more configuration options, such as the `flag` parameter. The most useful is `tabwriter.AlignRight`, which configures the writer to align the content to the right in each column.

Replacing part of the string

Another very common task related to string processing is the replacement of the substring in a string. Go standard library provide the `Replace` function and `Replacer` type for the replacement of multiple strings at once.

How to do it...

1. Open the console and create the folder `chapter02/recipe06`.
2. Navigate to the directory.
3. Create the `replace.go` file with the following content:

```go
package main

import (
 "fmt"
 "strings"
)

const refString = "Mary had a little lamb"
const refStringTwo = "lamb lamb lamb lamb"

func main() {
  out := strings.Replace(refString, "lamb", "wolf", -1)
  fmt.Println(out)

  out = strings.Replace(refStringTwo, "lamb", "wolf", 2)
  fmt.Println(out)
}
```

4. Run the code by executing `go run replace.go`.

5. See the output in the Terminal:

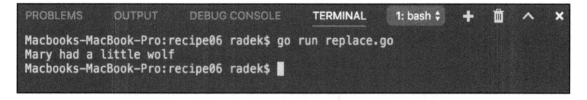

6. Create the `replacer.go` file with the following content:

```
package main

import (
    "fmt"
    "strings"
)

const refString = "Mary had a little lamb"

func main() {
    replacer := strings.NewReplacer("lamb", "wolf", "Mary", "Jack")
    out := replacer.Replace(refString)
    fmt.Println(out)
}
```

7. Run the code by executing `go run replacer.go`.

8. See the output in the Terminal:

```
PROBLEMS    OUTPUT    DEBUG CONSOLE    TERMINAL    1: bash ▾    +  🗑  ∧  ✕
Macbooks-MacBook-Pro:recipe06 radek$ go run replacer.go
Jack had a little wolf
Macbooks-MacBook-Pro:recipe06 radek$ ▊
```

9. Create the `regexp.go` file with the following content:

```
package main

import (
    "fmt"
    "regexp"
```

```
    )

    const refString = "Mary had a little lamb"

    func main() {
      regex := regexp.MustCompile("l[a-z]+")
      out := regex.ReplaceAllString(refString, "replacement")
      fmt.Println(out)
    }
```

10. Run the code by executing `go run regexp.go`.
11. See the output in the Terminal:

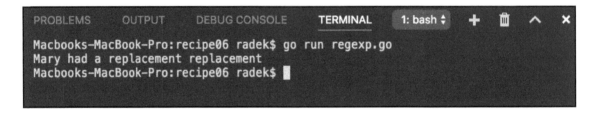

How it works...

The `Replace` function of a `strings` package is widely used for simple replacement. The last integer argument defines how many replacements will be done (in case of -1, all strings are replaced. See the second use of `Replace`, where only the first two occurrences are replaced.) The use of the `Replace` function is presented in steps **1 - 5**.

Besides the `Replace` function, the `Replacer` structure also has the `WriteString` method. This method will write to the given writer with all replacements defined in `Replacer`. The main purpose of this type is its reusability. It can replace multiple strings at once and it is safe for concurrent use; see steps **6 - 8**.

The more sophisticated method of replacing the substring, or even the matched pattern, is naturally the use of the regular expression. The `Regex` type pointer method `ReplaceAllString` could be leveraged for this purpose. Steps **9 - 11** illustrate the use of the `regexp` package.

There's more...

If more complex logic for the replacement is needed, the `regexp` package is probably the one that should be used.

Finding the substring in text by the regex pattern

There are always tasks such as validating the input, searching the document for any information, or even cleaning up a given string from unwanted escape characters. For these cases, regular expressions are usually used.

The Go standard library contains the `regexp` package, which covers the operations with regular expressions.

How to do it...

1. Open the console and create the folder `chapter02/recipe07`.
2. Navigate to the directory.
3. Create the `regexp.go` file with the following content:

```
package main

import (
  "fmt"
  "regexp"
)

const refString = `[{ \"email\": \"email@example.com\" \
                "phone\": 555467890},
               { \"email\": \"other@domain.com\" \
                "phone\": 555467890}]`

func main() {

  // This pattern is simplified for brevity
  emailRegexp := regexp.MustCompile("[a-zA-Z0-9]{1,}
                                    @[a-zA-Z0-9]{1,}\\.[a-z]{1,}")
  first := emailRegexp.FindString(refString)
  fmt.Println("First: ")
```

```
        fmt.Println(first)

        all := emailRegexp.FindAllString(refString, -1)
        fmt.Println("All: ")
        for _, val := range all {
          fmt.Println(val)
        }

    }
```

4. Run the code by executing the `go run regexp.go`.
5. See the output in the Terminal:

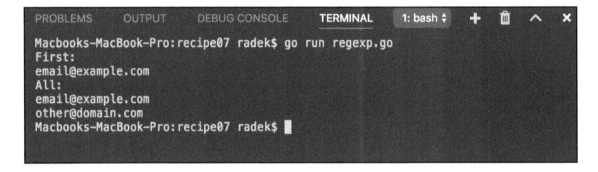

How it works...

The `FindString` or `FindAllString` functions are the simplest ways to find the matching pattern in the given string. The only difference is that the `FindString` method of `Regexp` will return only the first occurrence. On the other hand, the `FindAllString`, as the name suggests, returns a slice of strings with all occurrences.

The `Regexp` type offers a rich set of `FindXXX` methods. This recipe describes only the `String` variations that are usually most useful. Note that the preceding code uses the `MustCompile` function of the `regexp` package, which panics if the compilation of the regular expression fails.

See also

Besides this complex regular expression pattern matching, it is possible to match the substring only. This approach is described in the *Finding the substring in a string* recipe of this chapter.

Decoding a string from the non-Unicode charset

A lesser-known fact is that all content in .go files is encoded in UTF-8. Believe it or not the Unicode is not, the only charset in the world. For example, the Windows-1250 encoding is widely spread across Windows users.

When working with non-Unicode strings, you need to transcode the content to Unicode. This recipe demonstrates how to decode and encode the non-Unicode strings.

How to do it...

1. Open the console and create the folder chapter02/recipe08.
2. Navigate to the directory.
3. Create the file win1250.txt with content Gdańsk. The file must be encoded in the windows-1250 charset. If you are not sure how to do that, just jump to step 6 and after you complete step 7, which will create the windows-1250 encoded file, you can rename the out.txt file and go back to step 4.
4. Create the decode.go file with the following content:

```
package main

import (
  "fmt"
  "io/ioutil"
  "os"
  "strings"

  "golang.org/x/text/encoding/charmap"
)

func main() {
```

```go
  // Open windows-1250 file.
  f, err := os.Open("win1250.txt")
  if err != nil {
    panic(err)
  }
  defer f.Close()

  // Read all in raw form.
  b, err := ioutil.ReadAll(f)
  if err != nil {
    panic(err)
  }
  content := string(b)

  fmt.Println("Without decode: " + content)

  // Decode to unicode
  decoder := charmap.Windows1250.NewDecoder()
  reader := decoder.Reader(strings.NewReader(content))
  b, err = ioutil.ReadAll(reader)
  if err != nil {
    panic(err)
  }
  fmt.Println("Decoded: " + string(b))

}
```

5. Run the code by executing `go run decode.go`.
6. See the output in the Terminal:

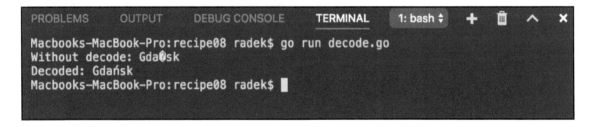

7. Create a file with the name `encode.go` with the following content:

```go
package main

import (
  "io"
  "os"
```

```
      "golang.org/x/text/encoding/charmap"
)

func main() {

   f, err := os.OpenFile("out.txt", os.O_CREATE|os.O_RDWR,
                           os.ModePerm|os.ModeAppend)
   if err != nil {
     panic(err)
   }
   defer f.Close()

   // Decode to unicode
   encoder := charmap.Windows1250.NewEncoder()
   writer := encoder.Writer(f)
   io.WriteString(writer, "Gdańsk")

}
```

8. Run the code by executing go run encode.go.
9. See the output in the file out.txt in Windows-1250 encoding and UTF-8 encoding.

How it works...

The package golang.org/x/text/encoding/charmap contains the Charset type for simple encoding and decoding. The type implements the NewDecoder method that creates the Decoder structure.

Steps **1 – 5** show the use of the decoding Reader.

The encoding works analogically. The encoding Writer is created and then each string written by this Writer is encoded into Windows-1250 encoding.

Note that the Windows-1250 was chosen as an example. The package, golang.org/x/text/encoding/charmap contains a lot of other charset options.

Controlling case

There are a lot of practical tasks where the modification of case is the most common approach. Let's pick a few of these:

- Case-insensitive comparison
- Beginning the sentence with an automatic first capital
- Camel-case to snake-case conversion

For these purposes, the `strings` package offers functions `ToLower`, `ToUpper`, `ToTitle`, and `Title`.

How to do it...

1. Open the console and create the folder `chapter02/recipe09`.
2. Navigate to the directory.
3. Create the `case.go` file with the following content:

```go
package main

import (
  "fmt"
  "strings"
  "unicode"
)

const email = "ExamPle@domain.com"
const name = "isaac newton"
const upc = "upc"
const i = "i"

const snakeCase = "first_name"

func main() {

  // For comparing the user input
  // sometimes it is better to
  // compare the input in a same
  // case.
  input := "Example@domain.com"
  input = strings.ToLower(input)
  emailToCompare := strings.ToLower(email)
```

```go
    matches := input == emailToCompare
    fmt.Printf("Email matches: %t\n", matches)

    upcCode := strings.ToUpper(upc)
    fmt.Println("UPPER case: " + upcCode)

    // This digraph has different upper case and
    // title case.
    str := "dz"
    fmt.Printf("%s in upper: %s and title: %s \n", str,
            strings.ToUpper(str), strings.ToTitle(str))

    // Use of XXXSpecial function
    title := strings.ToTitle(i)
    titleTurk := strings.ToTitleSpecial(unicode.TurkishCase, i)
    if title != titleTurk {
      fmt.Printf("ToTitle is defferent: %#U vs. %#U \n",
              title[0], []rune(titleTurk)[0])
    }

    // In some cases the input
    // needs to be corrected in case.
    correctNameCase := strings.Title(name)
    fmt.Println("Corrected name: " + correctNameCase)

    // Converting the snake case
    // to camel case with use of
    // Title and ToLower functions.
    firstNameCamel := toCamelCase(snakeCase)
    fmt.Println("Camel case: " + firstNameCamel)

}

func toCamelCase(input string) string {
  titleSpace := strings.Title(strings.Replace(input, "_", " ", -1))
  camel := strings.Replace(titleSpace, " ", "", -1)
  return strings.ToLower(camel[:1]) + camel[1:]
}
```

4. Run the code by executing `go run case.go`.

5. See the output in the Terminal:

```
PROBLEMS    OUTPUT    DEBUG CONSOLE    TERMINAL    2: bash ÷    +    ⬚    ⋀    ✕
Macbooks—MacBook-Pro:recipe09 radek$ go run case.go
Email matches: true
UPPER case: UPC
ǳ in upper: Ǳ and title: ǲ
ToTitle is defferent: U+0049 'I' vs. U+0130 'İ'
Corrected name: Isaac Newton
Camel case: firstName
Macbooks—MacBook-Pro:recipe09 radek$ ▮
```

How it works...

Note that the title-case mapping in Unicode differs from the uppercase mapping. The difference is that the number of characters requires special handling. These are mainly ligatures and digraphs such as *fl*, *dz*, and *lj*, plus a number of polytonic Greek characters. For example, *U+01C7 (LJ)* maps to *U+01C8 (Lj)* rather than to *U+01C9 (lj)*.

For proper case-insensitive comparison, the `EqualFold` function from the `strings` package should be used. This function uses case folding to normalize the strings and compare them.

Parsing comma-separated data

There are multiple table data formats. **CSV (comma-separated values)** is one of the most basic formats largely used for data transport and export. There is no standard that defines CSV, but the format itself is described in RFC 4180.

This recipe introduces how to parse CSV-formatted data comfortably.

How to do it...

1. Open the console and create the folder `chapter02/recipe10`.
2. Navigate to the directory.
3. Create a file named `data.csv` with the following content:

```
"Name","Surname","Age"
# this is comment in data
"John","Mnemonic",20
Maria,Tone,21
```

4. Create the `data.go` file with the following content:

```go
package main

import (
  "encoding/csv"
  "fmt"
  "os"
)

func main() {

    file, err := os.Open("data.csv")
    if err != nil {
      panic(err)
    }
    defer file.Close()

    reader := csv.NewReader(file)
    reader.FieldsPerRecord = 3
    reader.Comment = '#'

    for {
      record, e := reader.Read()
      if e != nil {
        fmt.Println(e)
        break
      }
      fmt.Println(record)
    }
}
```

5. Run the code by executing `go run data.go`.

6. See the output in the Terminal:

```
PROBLEMS    OUTPUT    DEBUG CONSOLE    TERMINAL    1: bash ⬍    ✚    🗑    ^    ✖
Macbooks-MacBook-Pro:recipe10 radek$ go run data.go
[Name Surname Age]
[John Mnemonic 20]
[Maria Tone 21]
EOF
Macbooks-MacBook-Pro:recipe10 radek$ ▊
```

7. Create a file named `data_uncommon.csv` with the following content:

```
Name;Surname;Age
"John";Mnemonic;20
"Maria";Tone;21
```

8. Create a file named `data_uncommon.go` with the following content:

```go
package main

import (
    "encoding/csv"
    "fmt"
    "os"
)

func main() {

    file, err := os.Open("data_uncommon.csv")
    if err != nil {
        panic(err)
    }
    defer file.Close()

    reader := csv.NewReader(file)
    reader.Comma = ';'

    for {
        record, e := reader.Read()
        if e != nil {
            fmt.Println(e)
            break
        }
```

```
        fmt.Println(record)
    }
}
```

9. Run the code by executing go run data_uncommon.go.

10. See the output in the Terminal:

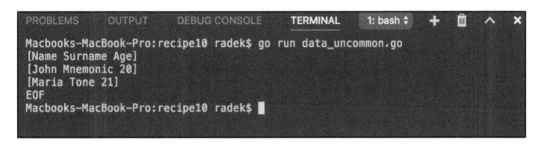

How it works...

Instead of simply scanning the input line by line and using strings.Split and other methods to parse the CSV format, Go offers a better way. The NewReader function in the encoding/csv package returns the Reader structure, which provides the API to read the CSV file. The Reader struct keeps variables to configure the read parameters, according to your needs.

The FieldsPerRecord parameter of Reader is a significant setting. This way the cell count per row could be validated. By default, when set to 0, it is set to the number of records in a first line. If a positive value is set, the number of records must match. If a negative value is set, there is no cell count validation.

Another interesting configuration is the Comment parameter, which allows you to define the comment characters in the parsed data. In the example, a whole line is ignored this way.

Go 1.10 now disallows the use of nonsensical comma and comment settings. This means null, carriage return, newline, invalid runes, and the Unicode replacement character. Also, setting comma and comment equal to each other is forbidden.

Managing whitespace in a string

The string input could contain too much whitespace, too little whitespace, or unsuitable whitespace chars. This recipe includes tips on how to manage these and format the string to your needs.

How to do it...

1. Open the console and create the folder `chapter02/recipe11`.
2. Navigate to the directory.
3. Create a file named `whitespace.go` with the following content:

```go
package main

import (
  "fmt"
  "math"
  "regexp"
  "strconv"
  "strings"
)

func main() {

  stringToTrim := "\t\t\n Go \tis\t Awesome \t\t"
  trimResult := strings.TrimSpace(stringToTrim)
  fmt.Println(trimResult)

  stringWithSpaces := "\t\t\n Go \tis\n Awesome \t\t"
  r := regexp.MustCompile("\\s+")
  replace := r.ReplaceAllString(stringWithSpaces, " ")
  fmt.Println(replace)

  needSpace := "need space"
  fmt.Println(pad(needSpace, 14, "CENTER"))
  fmt.Println(pad(needSpace, 14, "LEFT"))
}

func pad(input string, padLen int, align string) string {
  inputLen := len(input)

  if inputLen >= padLen {
    return input
```

```
    }

    repeat := padLen - inputLen
    var output string
    switch align {
      case "RIGHT":
        output = fmt.Sprintf("% "+strconv.Itoa(-padLen)+"s", input)
      case "LEFT":
        output = fmt.Sprintf("% "+strconv.Itoa(padLen)+"s", input)
      case "CENTER":
        bothRepeat := float64(repeat) / float64(2)
        left := int(math.Floor(bothRepeat)) + inputLen
        right := int(math.Ceil(bothRepeat))
        output = fmt.Sprintf("% "+strconv.Itoa(left)+"s%
                            "+strconv.Itoa(right)+"s", input, "")
    }
    return output
}
```

4. Run the code by executing `go run whitespace.go`.

5. See the output:

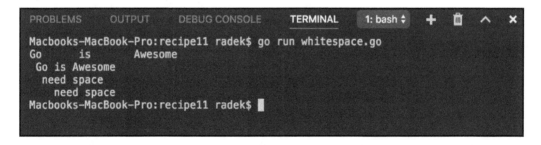

How it works...

Trimming the string before it is handled by the code is pretty common practice, and as the preceding code demonstrates, it is easily done by the standard Go library. The `strings` library also provides more variations of the `TrimXXX` function, which also allows the trimming of other chars from the string.

To trim the leading and ending whitespace, the `TrimSpace` function of the `strings` package can be used. This typifies the following part of a code, which was also included in the example earlier:

```
stringToTrim := "\t\t\n Go \tis\t Awesome \t\t"
stringToTrim = strings.TrimSpace(stringToTrim)
```

The `regex` package is suitable for replacing multiple spaces and tabs, and the string can be prepared for further processing this way. Note that, with this method, the break lines are replaced with a single space.

This part of the code represents the use of the regular expression to replace all multiple whitespaces with a single space:

```
r := regexp.MustCompile("\\s+")
replace := r.ReplaceAllString(stringToTrim, " ")
```

Padding is not an explicit function for the `strings` package, but it can be achieved by the `Sprintf` function of the `fmt` package. The `pad` function in code uses the formatting pattern `% <+/-padding>s` and some simple math to find out the padding. Finally, the minus sign before the padding number works as the right pad, and the positive number as the left pad.

See also

For more tips on how to work with regex, you can check the recipe, *Finding the substring in text by the regex pattern*, in this chapter.

Indenting a text document

The previous recipe depicts how to do string padding and whitespace trimming. This one will guide you through the indentation and unindentation of a text document. Similar principles from the previous recipes will be used.

How to do it...

1. Open the console and create the folder chapter02/recipe12.
2. Create the file main.go with the following content:

```go
package main

import (
  "fmt"
  "strconv"
  "strings"
  "unicode"
)

func main() {

  text := "Hi! Go is awesome."
  text = Indent(text, 6)
  fmt.Println(text)

  text = Unindent(text, 3)
  fmt.Println(text)

  text = Unindent(text, 10)
  fmt.Println(text)

  text = IndentByRune(text, 10, '.')
  fmt.Println(text)

}

// Indent indenting the input by given indent and rune
func IndentByRune(input string, indent int, r rune) string {
  return strings.Repeat(string(r), indent) + input
}

// Indent indenting the input by given indent
func Indent(input string, indent int) string {
  padding := indent + len(input)
  return fmt.Sprintf("% "+strconv.Itoa(padding)+"s", input)
}

// Unindent unindenting the input string. In case the
// input is indented by less than "indent" spaces
// the min of this both is removed.
func Unindent(input string, indent int) string {
```

```
count := 0
for _, val := range input {
  if unicode.IsSpace(val) {
    count++
  }
  if count == indent || !unicode.IsSpace(val) {
    break
  }
}

return input[count:]
}
```

3. Run the code by executing `go run main.go` in the Terminal.

4. See the output:

How it works...

The indentation is as simple as padding. In this case, the same formatting option is used. The more readable form of the `indent` implementation could use the `Repeat` function of the `strings` package. The `IndentByRune` function in the preceding code applies this approach.

Unindenting, in this case, means removing the given count of leading spaces. The implementation of `Unindent` in the preceding code removes the minimum number of leading spaces or given indentation.

See also

The *Managing whitespace in a string* recipe also works with spaces in a more generous way.

3
Dealing with Numbers

The recipes in this chapter are:

- Converting strings to numbers
- Comparing floating-point numbers
- Rounding floating-point numbers
- Floating-point arithmetics
- Formatting numbers
- Converting between binary, octal, decimal, and hexadecimal
- Formatting with the correct plurals
- Generating random numbers
- Operating complex numbers
- Converting between degrees and radians
- Taking logarithms
- Generating checksums

Introduction

The numbers are generally the inevitable part of each application—printing the formatted numbers, converting base representations, and so on. This chapter presents a lot of operations that you can commonly deal with.

Check if Go is properly installed. The *Getting ready* section from the *Retrieving Golang version* recipe of `Chapter 1`, *Interacting With Environment*, will help you.

Converting strings to numbers

This recipe will show you how to convert the strings containing numbers to a numeric type (integer or floating-point value).

How to do it...

1. Open the console and create the folder `chapter03/recipe01`.
2. Navigate to the directory.
3. Create the `main.go` file with the following content:

```go
package main

import (
  "fmt"
  "strconv"
)

const bin = "00001"
const hex = "2f"
const intString = "12"
const floatString = "12.3"

func main() {

  // Decimals
  res, err := strconv.Atoi(intString)
  if err != nil {
    panic(err)
  }
  fmt.Printf("Parsed integer: %d\n", res)

  // Parsing hexadecimals
  res64, err := strconv.ParseInt(hex, 16, 32)
  if err != nil {
    panic(err)
  }
  fmt.Printf("Parsed hexadecima: %d\n", res64)

  // Parsing binary values
  resBin, err := strconv.ParseInt(bin, 2, 32)
  if err != nil {
    panic(err)
```

```
}
fmt.Printf("Parsed bin: %d\n", resBin)

// Parsing floating-points
resFloat, err := strconv.ParseFloat(floatString, 32)
if err != nil {
  panic(err)
}
fmt.Printf("Parsed float: %.5f\n", resFloat)

}
```

4. Execute the command go run main.go in the Terminal.

5. You will see the following output:

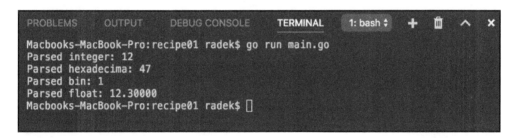

How it works...

The dominant function in the preceding sample code is the ParseInt function of package strconv. The function is called with three arguments: input, the base of input, and bit size. The base determines how the number is parsed. Note that the hexadecimal has the base (second argument) of 16 and the binary has the base of 2. The function Atoi of package strconv is, in fact, the ParseInt function with the base of 10.

The ParseFloat function converts the string to a floating-point number. The second argument is the precision of bitSize. bitSize = 64 will result in float64. bitSize = 32 will result in float64, but it is convertible to float32 without changing its value.

Comparing floating-point numbers

Because of how floating-point numbers are represented, there can be inconsistencies while comparing two numbers that appear to be identical. Unlike integers, IEEE floating-point numbers are only approximated. The need to convert the numbers to a form the computer can store in binary leads to minor precision or round-off deviations. For example, a value of 1.3 could be represented as 1.29999999999. The comparison could be done with some tolerance. To compare numbers with arbitrary precision, the `big` package is here.

How to do it...

1. Open the console and create the folder `chapter03/recipe02`.
2. Navigate to the directory.
3. Create the `tolerance.go` file with the following content:

```go
package main

import (
  "fmt"
  "math"
)

const da = 0.29999999999999998889776975374843459576368331909180
const db = 0.3

func main() {

  daStr := fmt.Sprintf("%.10f", da)
  dbStr := fmt.Sprintf("%.10f", db)

  fmt.Printf("Strings %s = %s equals: %v \n", daStr,
        dbStr, dbStr == daStr)
  fmt.Printf("Number equals: %v \n", db == da)

  // As the precision of float representation
  // is limited. For the float comparison it is
  // better to use comparison with some tolerance.
  fmt.Printf("Number equals with TOLERANCE: %v \n",
        equals(da, db))

}

const TOLERANCE = 1e-8
```

```go
// Equals compares the floating-point numbers
// with tolerance 1e-8
func equals(numA, numB float64) bool {
  delta := math.Abs(numA - numB)
  if delta < TOLERANCE {
    return true
  }
  return false
}
```

4. Execute the command `go run tolerance.go` in the Terminal.

5. You will see the following output:

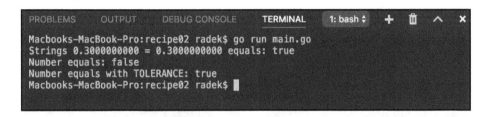

6. Create the file `big.go` with the following content:

```go
package main

import (
  "fmt"
  "math/big"
)

var da float64 = 0.299999992
var db float64 = 0.299999991

var prec uint = 32
var prec2 uint = 16

func main() {

  fmt.Printf("Comparing float64 with '==' equals: %v\n", da == db)

  daB := big.NewFloat(da).SetPrec(prec)
  dbB := big.NewFloat(db).SetPrec(prec)

  fmt.Printf("A: %v \n", daB)
  fmt.Printf("B: %v \n", dbB)
  fmt.Printf("Comparing big.Float with precision: %d : %v\n",
```

```
                    prec, daB.Cmp(dbB) == 0)

        daB = big.NewFloat(da).SetPrec(prec2)
        dbB = big.NewFloat(db).SetPrec(prec2)

        fmt.Printf("A: %v \n", daB)
        fmt.Printf("B: %v \n", dbB)
        fmt.Printf("Comparing big.Float with precision: %d : %v\n",
                    prec2, daB.Cmp(dbB) == 0)

    }
```

7. Execute the code by running `go run big.go` in the Terminal.
8. You will see the following output:

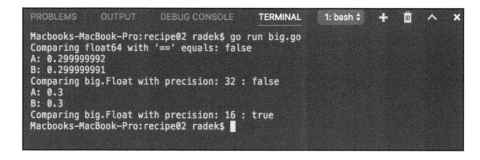

How it works...

The first approach for the floating-point numbers comparison without the use of any built-in package (steps **1-5**) requires the use of a so-called EPSILON constant. This is the value chosen to be a sufficient small delta (difference) between two numbers to consider the values as equal. The delta constant could be on the order of 1e-8, which is usually sufficient precision.

The second option is more complex, but also more useful for further work with floating-point numbers. The package `math/big` offers the `Float` type that could be configured for a given precision. The advantage of this package is that the precision could be much higher than the precision of the `float64` type. For illustrative purposes, the small precision values were used to show the rounding and comparison in the given precision.

Note that the `da` and `db` numbers are equal when using the precision of 16-bits and not equal when using the precision of 32-bits. The maximal configurable precision can be obtained from the `big.MaxPrec` constant.

Rounding floating-point numbers

The rounding of a floating-point number to an integer or to a particular precision has to be done properly. The most common error is to cast the floating-point type `float64` to an integer type and consider it as well-handled.

An example could be casting the number 3.9999 to an integer and expect it to become an integer of value 4. The real result would be 3. At the time of writing this book, the current version of Go (1.9.2) does not contain the `Round` function. However, in version 1.10, the `Round` function was already implemented in the `math` package.

How to do it...

1. Open the console and create the folder `chapter03/recipe03`.
2. Navigate to the directory.
3. Create the `round.go` file with the following content:

```
package main

import (
  "fmt"
  "math"
)

var valA float64 = 3.55554444

func main() {

  // Bad assumption on rounding
  // the number by casting it to
  // integer.
  intVal := int(valA)
  fmt.Printf("Bad rounding by casting to int: %v\n", intVal)

  fRound := Round(valA)
  fmt.Printf("Rounding by custom function: %v\n", fRound)

}

// Round returns the nearest integer.
func Round(x float64) float64 {
  t := math.Trunc(x)
  if math.Abs(x-t) >= 0.5 {
```

```
        return t + math.Copysign(1, x)
    }
    return t
}
```

4. Execute the code by running `go run round.go` in the Terminal.
5. You will see the following output:

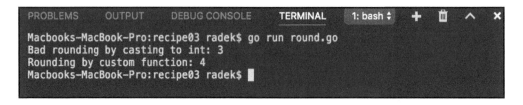

```
PROBLEMS      OUTPUT      DEBUG CONSOLE      TERMINAL      1: bash ⬍    +   🗑   ⌃   ✕
Macbooks-MacBook-Pro:recipe03 radek$ go run round.go
Bad rounding by casting to int: 3
Rounding by custom function: 4
Macbooks-MacBook-Pro:recipe03 radek$ ▌
```

How it works...

Casting the float to integer actually just truncates the float value. Let's say the value 2 is represented as 1.999999; in this case, the output would be 1, which is not what you expected.

The proper way of rounding the float number is to use the function that would also consider the decimal part. The commonly used method of rounding is to half away from zero (also known as commercial rounding). Put simply, if the number contains the absolute value of the decimal part which is greater or equal to 0.5, the number is rounded up, otherwise, it is rounded down.

In the function `Round`, the function `Trunc` of package `math` truncates the decimal part of the number. Then, the decimal part of the number is extracted. If the value exceeds the limit of 0.5 than the value of 1 with the same sign as the integer value is added.

Go version 1.10 uses a faster implementation of the function mentioned in the example. In version 1.10, you can just call the `math.Round` function to get the rounded number.

Floating-point arithmetics

As described in previous recipes, the representation of the floating-point numbers also complicates the arithmetic. For general purposes, the operations on the built-in `float64` are sufficient. In case more precision is needed, the `math/big` package comes into play. This recipe will show you how to handle this.

How to do it...

1. Open the console and create the folder `chapter03/recipe04`.
2. Navigate to the directory.
3. Create the `main.go` file with the following content:

```
package main

import (
  "fmt"
  "math/big"
)

const PI = `3.14159265358979323846264338327950288419716939
          9375105820974944592307816406286208998628034825
          3421170679821480865132823066470938446095505822317
          25359408128481117450284102701938521105559644629
          4895493038196`
const diameter = 3.0
const precision = 400

func main() {

  pi, _ := new(big.Float).SetPrec(precision).SetString(PI)
  d := new(big.Float).SetPrec(precision).SetFloat64(diameter)

  circumference := new(big.Float).Mul(pi, d)

  pi64, _ := pi.Float64()
  fmt.Printf("Circumference big.Float = %.400f\n",
          circumference)
  fmt.Printf("Circumference float64 = %.400f\n", pi64*diameter)

  sum := new(big.Float).Add(pi, pi)
  fmt.Printf("Sum = %.400f\n", sum)
```

```go
    diff := new(big.Float).Sub(pi, pi)
    fmt.Printf("Diff = %.400f\n", diff)

    quo := new(big.Float).Quo(pi, pi)
    fmt.Printf("Quocient = %.400f\n", quo)

}
```

4. Execute the code by running `go run main.go` in the Terminal.
5. You will see the following output:

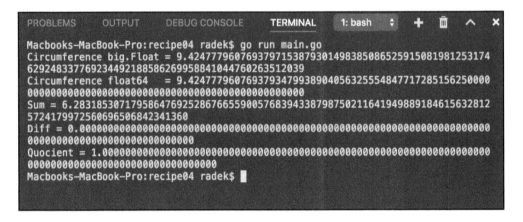

How it works...

The `big` package provides support for the arithmetic of floating-point numbers with high precision. The previous example illustrates the basic operations over the numbers. Note that the code compares the operation with the `float64` type and the `big.Float` type.

By working with numbers with a high precision, it is crucial to use the `big.Float` type. When `big.Float` is converted back to the built-in `float64` type, high precision is lost.

There's more...

The big package contains more operations of the `Float` type. See the documentation (`https://golang.org/pkg/math/big/#Float`) of this package for more details.

See also

The comparison and rounding of floating-point numbers is mentioned in the *Comparing floating-point numbers* and *Rounding floating-point numbers* recipes.

Formatting numbers

If the numbers are converted to the string, they usually need to be reasonably formatted. The formatting of a number means the number is printed with a given number, made up of digits and decimals. The representation of a value can also be chosen. A closely related problem with this, however, is the localization of number formatting. For example, some languages use comma-separated zeros.

How to do it...

1. Open the console and create the folder `chapter03/recipe05`.
2. Navigate to the directory.
3. Create the `format.go` file with the following content:

```go
package main

import (
  "fmt"
)

var integer int64 = 32500
var floatNum float64 = 22000.456

func main() {

  // Common way how to print the decimal
  // number
  fmt.Printf("%d \n", integer)

  // Always show the sign
  fmt.Printf("%+d \n", integer)

  // Print in other base X -16, o-8, b -2, d - 10
  fmt.Printf("%X \n", integer)
  fmt.Printf("%#X \n", integer)
```

```go
	// Padding with leading zeros
	fmt.Printf("%010d \n", integer)

	// Left padding with spaces
	fmt.Printf("% 10d \n", integer)

	// Right padding
	fmt.Printf("% -10d \n", integer)

	// Print floating
	// point number
	fmt.Printf("%f \n", floatNum)

	// Floating-point number
	// with limited precision = 5
	fmt.Printf("%.5f \n", floatNum)

	// Floating-point number
	// in scientific notation
	fmt.Printf("%e \n", floatNum)

	// Floating-point number
	// %e for large exponents
	// or %f otherwise
	fmt.Printf("%g \n", floatNum)

}
```

4. Execute the code by running `go run format.go` in the main Terminal.
5. You will see the following output:

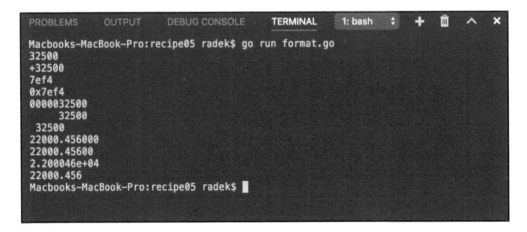

6. Create the file `localized.go` with the following content:

```
package main

import (
    "golang.org/x/text/language"
    "golang.org/x/text/message"
)

const num = 100000.5678

func main() {
    p := message.NewPrinter(language.English)
    p.Printf(" %.2f \n", num)

    p = message.NewPrinter(language.German)
    p.Printf(" %.2f \n", num)
}
```

7. Execute the code by running `go run localized.go` in the main Terminal.
8. You will see the following output:

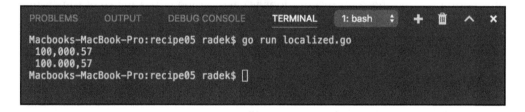

How it works...

The code example shows the most commonly used options for integers and floating-point numbers.

> The formatting in Go is derived from C's `printf` function. The so-called `verbs` are used to define the formatting of a number. The verb, for example, could be `%X`, which in fact is a placeholder for the value.

Besides the basic formatting, there are also rules in formatting that are related to the local manners. With formatting, according to the locale, the package golang.org/x/text/message could help. See the second code example in this recipe. This way, it is possible to localize the number formatting.

There's more...

For all formatting options, see the fmt package. The strconv package could also be useful in case you are looking to format numbers in a different base. The following recipe describes the possibility of number conversion, but as a side effect, the options of how to format numbers in a different base are presented.

Converting between binary, octal, decimal, and hexadecimal

In some cases, the integer values can be represented by other than decimal representations. The conversion between these representations is easily done with the use of the strconv package.

How to do it...

1. Open the console and create the folder chapter03/recipe06.
2. Navigate to the directory.
3. Create the convert.go file with the following content:

```
package main

import (
  "fmt"
  "strconv"
)

const bin = "10111"
const hex = "1A"
const oct = "12"
const dec = "10"
const floatNum = 16.123557
```

```go
func main() {

    // Converts binary value into hex
    v, _ := ConvertInt(bin, 2, 16)
    fmt.Printf("Binary value %s converted to hex: %s\n", bin, v)

    // Converts hex value into dec
    v, _ = ConvertInt(hex, 16, 10)
    fmt.Printf("Hex value %s converted to dec: %s\n", hex, v)

    // Converts oct value into hex
    v, _ = ConvertInt(oct, 8, 16)
    fmt.Printf("Oct value %s converted to hex: %s\n", oct, v)

    // Converts dec value into oct
    v, _ = ConvertInt(dec, 10, 8)
    fmt.Printf("Dec value %s converted to oct: %s\n", dec, v)

    //... analogically any other conversion
    // could be done.

}

// ConvertInt converts the given string value of base
// to defined toBase.
func ConvertInt(val string, base, toBase int) (string, error) {
    i, err := strconv.ParseInt(val, base, 64)
    if err != nil {
        return "", err
    }
    return strconv.FormatInt(i, toBase), nil
}
```

4. Execute the code by running `go run convert.go` in the main Terminal.
5. You will see the following output:

```
PROBLEMS    OUTPUT    DEBUG CONSOLE    TERMINAL    1: bash
Macbooks-MacBook-Pro:recipe06 radek$ go run convert.go
Binary value 10111 converted to hex: 17
Hex value 1A converted to dec: 26
Oct value 12 converted to hex: a
Dec value 10 converted to oct: 12
Macbooks-MacBook-Pro:recipe06 radek$
```

How it works...

The `strconv` package provides the functions `ParseInt` and `FormatInt` which are the, let's say, complementary functions. The function `ParseInt` is able to parse the integer number in any base representation. The function `FormatInt`, on the other hand, can format the integer into any given base.

Finally, it is possible to parse the string representation of the integer to the built-in `int64` type and subsequently, format the string of the parsed integer into the given base representation.

Formatting with the correct plurals

When displaying messages for the user, the interaction is more pleasant if the sentences feel more human. The Go package `golang.org/x/text`, which is the extension package, contains this feature for formatting plurals in the correct way.

Getting ready

Execute `go get -x golang.org/x/text` to obtain the extension package in case you don't have it already.

How to do it...

1. Open the console and create the folder `chapter03/recipe07`.
2. Navigate to the directory.
3. Create the `plurals.go` file with the following content:

```
package main

import (
  "golang.org/x/text/feature/plural"
  "golang.org/x/text/language"
  "golang.org/x/text/message"
)

func main() {
```

```
message.Set(language.English, "%d items to do",
  plural.Selectf(1, "%d", "=0", "no items to do",
    plural.One, "one item to do",
    "<100", "%[1]d items to do",
    plural.Other, "lot of items to do",
))

message.Set(language.English, "The average is %.2f",
  plural.Selectf(1, "%.2f",
    "<1", "The average is zero",
    "=1", "The average is one",
    plural.Other, "The average is %[1]f ",
))

prt := message.NewPrinter(language.English)
prt.Printf("%d items to do", 0)
prt.Println()
prt.Printf("%d items to do", 1)
prt.Println()
prt.Printf("%d items to do", 10)
prt.Println()
prt.Printf("%d items to do", 1000)
prt.Println()

prt.Printf("The average is %.2f", 0.8)
prt.Println()
prt.Printf("The average is %.2f", 1.0)
prt.Println()
prt.Printf("The average is %.2f", 10.0)
prt.Println()

}
```

4. Execute the code by running `go run plurals.go` in the main Terminal.

5. You will see the following output:

```
PROBLEMS    OUTPUT    DEBUG CONSOLE    TERMINAL    1: bash

Macbooks-MacBook-Pro:recipe07 radek$ go run plurals.go
no items to do
one item to do
10 items to do
lot of items to do
The average is zero
The average is one
The average is 10.000000
Macbooks-MacBook-Pro:recipe07 radek$
```

How it works...

The package `golang.org/x/text/message` contains the function `NewPrinter` which accepts the language identification and creates the formatted I/O, the same as the `fmt` package does, but with the ability to translate messages based on gender and plural forms.

The `Set` function of the `message` package adds the translation and plurals selection. The plural form itself is selected based on rules set via the `Selectf` function. The `Selectf` function produces the `catalog.Message` type with rules based on the `plural.Form` or selector.

The preceding sample code uses `plural.One` and `plural.Other` forms, and `=x`, `<x` selectors. These are matched against the formatting verb `%d` (other verbs can also be used). The first matching case is chosen.

There's more...

For more information about the selectors and forms, see the documentation for the `golang.org/x/text/message` package.

Generating random numbers

This recipe shows how to generate random numbers. This functionality is provided by the `math/rand` package. The random numbers generated by `math/rand` are considered cryptographically insecure because the sequences are repeatable with given seed.

To generate cryptographically secure numbers, the `crypto/rand` package should be used. These sequences are not repeatable.

How to do it...

1. Open the console and create the folder `chapter03/recipe08`.
2. Navigate to the directory.
3. Create the `rand.go` file with the following content:

```go
package main

import (
  crypto "crypto/rand"
  "fmt"
  "math/big"
  "math/rand"
)

func main() {

  sec1 := rand.New(rand.NewSource(10))
  sec2 := rand.New(rand.NewSource(10))
  for i := 0; i < 5; i++ {
    rnd1 := sec1.Int()
    rnd2 := sec2.Int()
    if rnd1 != rnd2 {
      fmt.Println("Rand generated non-equal sequence")
      break
    } else {
      fmt.Printf("Math/Rand1: %d , Math/Rand2: %d\n", rnd1, rnd2)
    }
  }

  for i := 0; i < 5; i++ {
    safeNum := NewCryptoRand()
    safeNum2 := NewCryptoRand()
```

```
    if safeNum == safeNum2 {
      fmt.Println("Crypto generated equal numbers")
      break
    } else {
      fmt.Printf("Crypto/Rand1: %d , Crypto/Rand2: %d\n",
                 safeNum, safeNum2)
    }
  }
}

func NewCryptoRand() int64 {
  safeNum, err := crypto.Int(crypto.Reader, big.NewInt(100234))
  if err != nil {
    panic(err)
  }
  return safeNum.Int64()
}
```

4. Execute the code by running `go run rand.go` in the main Terminal.
5. You will see the following output:

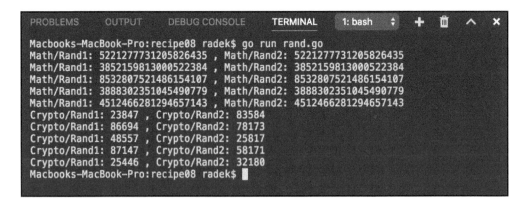

How it works...

The previous code presents two possibilities on how to generate random numbers. The first option uses the `math/rand` package, which is cryptographically insecure, and allows us to generate the same sequence with the use of `Source` with the same seed number. This approach is usually used in tests. The reason for doing so is for the reproducibility of the sequence.

The second option, the cryptographically secure one, is the use of the `crypto/rand` package. The API uses the `Reader` to provide the instance of a cryptographically strong pseudo-random generator. The package itself has the default `Reader` which is usually based on the system-based random number generator.

Operating complex numbers

Complex numbers are usually used for scientific applications and calculations. Go implements complex numbers as the primitive type. The specific operations on complex numbers are part of the `math/cmplx` package.

How to do it...

1. Open the console and create the folder `chapter03/recipe09`.
2. Navigate to the directory.
3. Create the `complex.go` file with the following content:

```go
package main

import (
    "fmt"
    "math/cmplx"
)

func main() {

    // complex numbers are
    // defined as real and imaginary
    // part defined by float64
    a := complex(2, 3)

    fmt.Printf("Real part: %f \n", real(a))
    fmt.Printf("Complex part: %f \n", imag(a))

    b := complex(6, 4)

    // All common
    // operators are useful
    c := a - b
    fmt.Printf("Difference : %v\n", c)
    c = a + b
```

```
fmt.Printf("Sum : %v\n", c)
c = a * b
fmt.Printf("Product : %v\n", c)
c = a / b
fmt.Printf("Product : %v\n", c)

conjugate := cmplx.Conj(a)
fmt.Println("Complex number a's conjugate : ", conjugate)

cos := cmplx.Cos(b)
fmt.Println("Cosine of b : ", cos)


}
```

4. Execute the code by running `go run complex.go` in the main Terminal.
5. You will see the following output:

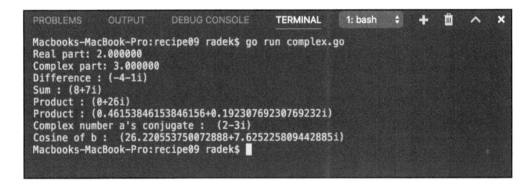

How it works...

The basic operators are implemented for the primitive type `complex`. The other operations on complex numbers are provided by the `math/cmplx` package. In case high precision operations are needed, there is no `big` implementation.

On the other hand, the complex number could be implemented as real, and the imaginary part expressed by the `big.Float` type.

Converting between degrees and radians

The trigonometric operations and geometric manipulation are usually done in radians; it is always useful to be able to convert these into degrees and vice versa. This recipe will show you some tips on how to handle the conversion between these units.

How to do it...

1. Open the console and create the folder `chapter03/recipe10`.
2. Navigate to the directory.
3. Create the `radians.go` file with the following content:

```go
package main

import (
  "fmt"
  "math"
)

type Radian float64

func (rad Radian) ToDegrees() Degree {
  return Degree(float64(rad) * (180.0 / math.Pi))
}

func (rad Radian) Float64() float64 {
  return float64(rad)
}

type Degree float64

func (deg Degree) ToRadians() Radian {
  return Radian(float64(deg) * (math.Pi / 180.0))
}

func (deg Degree) Float64() float64 {
  return float64(deg)
}

func main() {

  val := radiansToDegrees(1)
  fmt.Printf("One radian is : %.4f degrees\n", val)
```

```go
    val2 := degreesToRadians(val)
    fmt.Printf("%.4f degrees is %.4f rad\n", val, val2)

    // Conversion as part
    // of type methods
    val = Radian(1).ToDegrees().Float64()
    fmt.Printf("Degrees: %.4f degrees\n", val)

    val = Degree(val).ToRadians().Float64()
    fmt.Printf("Rad: %.4f radians\n", val)
}

func degreesToRadians(deg float64) float64 {
    return deg * (math.Pi / 180.0)
}

func radiansToDegrees(rad float64) float64 {
    return rad * (180.0 / math.Pi)
}
```

4. Execute the code by running `go run radians.go` in the main Terminal.
5. You will see the following output:

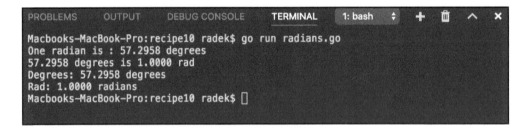

How it works...

The Go standard library does not contain any package with a function converting radians to degrees and vice versa. But at least the Pi constant is a part of the `math` package, so the conversion could be done as shown in the sample code.

The preceding code also presents the approach of defining the custom type with additional methods. These are simplifying the conversion of values by handy API.

Taking logarithms

Logarithms are used in scientific applications as well as in data visualizations and measurements. The built-in math package contains the commonly used bases of the logarithm. Using these, you are able to get all bases.

How to do it...

1. Open the console and create the folder chapter03/recipe11.
2. Navigate to the directory.
3. Create the log.go file with the following content:

```
package main

import (
  "fmt"
  "math"
)

func main() {

  ln := math.Log(math.E)
  fmt.Printf("Ln(E) = %.4f\n", ln)

  log10 := math.Log10(-100)
  fmt.Printf("Log10(10) = %.4f\n", log10)

  log2 := math.Log2(2)
  fmt.Printf("Log2(2) = %.4f\n", log2)

  log_3_6 := Log(3, 6)
  fmt.Printf("Log3(6) = %.4f\n", log_3_6)

}

// Log computes the logarithm of
// base > 1 and x greater 0
func Log(base, x float64) float64 {
  return math.Log(x) / math.Log(base)
}
```

4. Execute the code by running `go run log.go` in the main Terminal.

5. You will see the following output:

```
PROBLEMS    OUTPUT    DEBUG CONSOLE    TERMINAL    1: bash  ⇕    +  🗑  ∧  ✕
Macbooks-MacBook-Pro:recipe11 radek$ go run log.go
Ln(E) = 1.0000
Log10(10) = NaN
Log2(2) = 1.0000
Log3(6) = 1.6309
Macbooks-MacBook-Pro:recipe11 radek$ ▊
```

How it works...

The standard package, `math`, contains functions for all commonly used logarithms, and so you can easily get binary, decimal, and natural logarithms. See the *Log* function which counts any logarithm of *y* with base *x* through the helper-defined formula:

$$Log_x(y) = \frac{Ln(y)}{Ln(x)}$$

The internal implementation of the logarithm in standard lib is naturally based on approximation. This function can be seen in the `$GOROOT/src/math/log.go` file.

Generating checksums

The hash, or so-called checksum, is the easiest way to quickly compare any content. This recipe demonstrates how to create the checksum of the file content. For demonstration purposes, the MD5 hash function will be used.

How to do it...

1. Open the console and create the folder `chapter03/recipe12`.

2. Navigate to the directory.

3. Create the `content.dat` file with the following content:

```
This is content to check
```

4. Create the `checksum.go` file with the following content:

```go
package main

import (
  "crypto/md5"
  "fmt"
  "io"
  "os"
)

var content = "This is content to check"

func main() {

  checksum := MD5(content)
  checksum2 := FileMD5("content.dat")

  fmt.Printf("Checksum 1: %s\n", checksum)
  fmt.Printf("Checksum 2: %s\n", checksum2)
  if checksum == checksum2 {
    fmt.Println("Content matches!!!")
  }

}

// MD5 creates the md5
// hash for given content encoded in
// hex string
func MD5(data string) string {
  h := md5.Sum([]byte(data))
  return fmt.Sprintf("%x", h)
}

// FileMD5 creates hex encoded md5 hash
// of file content
func FileMD5(path string) string {
  h := md5.New()
  f, err := os.Open(path)
  if err != nil {
    panic(err)
  }
  defer f.Close()
```

```
    _, err = io.Copy(h, f)
    if err != nil {
      panic(err)
    }
    return fmt.Sprintf("%x", h.Sum(nil))
  }
```

5. Execute the code by running `go run checksum.go` in the main Terminal.

6. You will see the following output:

7. Create the `sha_panic.go` file with the following content:

```
package main

import (
  "crypto"
)

func main() {
  crypto.SHA1.New()
}
```

8. Execute the code by running `go run sha_panic.go` in the main Terminal.

9. You will see the following output:

```
PROBLEMS    OUTPUT    DEBUG CONSOLE    TERMINAL    1: bash

Macbooks-MacBook-Pro:recipe12 radek$ go run sha_panic.go
panic: crypto: requested hash function #3 is unavailable

goroutine 1 [running]:
crypto.Hash.New(0x3, 0xc420041f70, 0x1050d14)
        /Users/radek/Software/Go/1.9.2/src/crypto/crypto.go:89 +0x110
main.main()
        /Users/radek/Projects/Packt_Publishing/GoStdLibCookbook/Dealing With Num
bers/recipe12/sha_panic.go:8 +0x2a
exit status 2
Macbooks-MacBook-Pro:recipe12 radek$ []
```

How it works...

The `crypto` package contains implementations of well-known hash functions. The MD5 hash function is located in the `crypto/md5` package. Each hash function in the `crypto` package implements the `Hash` interface. Note that `Hash` contains the `Write` method. With the `Write` method, it can be utilized as a `Writer`. This can be seen in the `FileMD5` function. The `Sum` method of `Hash` accepts the argument of byte slice, where the resulting hash should be placed.

Beware of this. The `Sum` method does not compute the hash of the argument, but computes the hash into an argument.

On the other hand, `md5.Sum`, the package function, can be used to produce the hash directly. In this case, the argument of the `Sum` function is the one from the hash values computed.

Naturally, the `crypto` package implements the SHA variants and other hash functions as well. These are usually used in the same way. The hash functions can be accessed through the `crypto` package constant `crypto.Hash` (for example, `crypto.MD5.New()`), but this way, the package with the given function must be linked to a built binary as well (the blank import could be used, `import _ "crypto/md5"`), otherwise the call for `New` will panic.

The `hash` package itself contains the CRC checksums and more.

4
Once Upon a Time

The recipes in this chapter are:

- Finding today's date
- Formatting date to string
- Parsing the string into date
- Converting dates to epoch and vice versa
- Retrieving time units from the date
- Date arithmetics
- Finding the difference between two dates
- Converting between time zones
- Running the code block periodically
- Waiting a certain amount of time
- Timeout long-running operations
- Serializing the time and date

Introduction

This chapter is all about time-related tasks and operations. Go concentrates all these in the standard package called `time`. With this package, you are able to obtain the current time and date, format the date to the string, convert time zones, create timers, and create tickers. Keep in mind that there are always many ways you can implement and design functionality, and this chapter will show only a few of them.

Verify whether Go is installed properly. In case of any issues, see the *Retrieving Golang version* recipe in `Chapter 1`, *Interacting With the Environment*, and follow the steps of the *Getting ready* section.

Finding today's date

Obtaining the current date is a very common task for any system or application. Let's look at how this is done with help of Go's standard library.

How to do it...

1. Open the console and create the folder `chapter04/recipe01`.
2. Navigate to the directory.
3. Create the `today.go` file with the following content:

```
package main

import (
  "fmt"
  "time"
)

func main() {
  today := time.Now()
  fmt.Println(today)
}
```

4. Execute the code by running `go run today.go` in the main Terminal.
5. You will see the following output:

How it works...

The built-in package `time` contains the function `Now`, which provides the instance of a `Time` initialized to the current local time and date.

The `Time` type is an instant in time in nanoseconds. The zero value of `Time` is January 1, year 1, 00:00:00.000000000 UTC.

The pointer to the `Time` type should not be used. If only the value (not pointer to variable) is used, the `Time` instance is considered to be safe for use across multiple goroutines. The only exception is with serialization.

See also

For more information on the `Time` type, see the `time` package documentation at: `https://golang.org/pkg/time`.

Formatting date to string

In case the textual representation of a time value is needed, usually, certain formatting is expected. The `Time` type of the `time` package provides the ability to create the `string` output in the given format. There are some rules on how to do this and we will cover a few useful ones.

How to do it...

1. Open the console and create the folder `chapter04/recipe02`.
2. Navigate to the directory.
3. Create the `format.go` file with the following content:

```
package main

import (
  "fmt"
  "time"
)

func main() {
  tTime := time.Date(2017, time.March, 5, 8, 5, 2, 0, time.Local)

  // The formatting is done
  // with use of reference value
  // Jan 2 15:04:05 2006 MST
  fmt.Printf("tTime is: %s\n", tTime.Format("2006/1/2"))

  fmt.Printf("The time is: %s\n", tTime.Format("15:04"))
```

```
        //The predefined formats could
        // be used
        fmt.Printf("The time is: %s\n", tTime.Format(time.RFC1123))

        // The formatting supports space padding
        //only for days in Go version 1.9.2
        fmt.Printf("tTime is: %s\n", tTime.Format("2006/1/_2"))

        // The zero padding is done by adding 0
        fmt.Printf("tTime is: %s\n", tTime.Format("2006/01/02"))

        //The fraction with leading zeros use 0s
        fmt.Printf("tTime is: %s\n", tTime.Format("15:04:05.00"))

        //The fraction without leading zeros use 9s
        fmt.Printf("tTime is: %s\n", tTime.Format("15:04:05.999"))

        // Append format appends the formatted time to given
        // buffer
        fmt.Println(string(tTime.AppendFormat([]byte("The time
                    is up: "), "03:04PM")))
    }
```

4. Execute the code by running `go run format.go` in the main Terminal.
5. You will see the following output:

How it works...

The `Time` type of the `time` package provides the `Format` method for formatting the output string.

Go uses the referential time value `Jan 2 15:04:05 2006 MST` to define the formatting layout. See the code example for padding options.

> The memo for the reference date is that when given in number form, it is represented as 1,2,3,4,5,6,-7. The -7 value means that the MST time zone is 7 hours behind the UTC.

The time package includes some predefined formats (for example, `time.Kitchen`); you can discover these in the documentation for package constants. (`https://golang.org/pkg/time/#pkg-constants`)

See also

For all predefined formats and formatting options, see the documentation for the `time` package at: `https://golang.org/pkg/time`.

Parsing the string into date

The same concept as the one used in date formatting is also used by date parsing. The same reference date and layout principles can be used. This recipe will show you how to transform the string input into a `Time` instance.

How to do it...

1. Open the console and create the folder `chapter04/recipe03`.
2. Navigate to the directory.
3. Create the `parse.go` file with the following content:

```
package main

import (
  "fmt"
  "time"
)

func main() {
```

```
    // If timezone is not defined
    // than Parse function returns
    // the time in UTC timezone.
    t, err := time.Parse("2/1/2006", "31/7/2015")
    if err != nil {
      panic(err)
    }
    fmt.Println(t)

    // If timezone is given than it is parsed
    // in given timezone
    t, err = time.Parse("2/1/2006 3:04 PM MST",
                        "31/7/2015 1:25 AM DST")
    if err != nil {
      panic(err)
    }
    fmt.Println(t)

    // Note that the ParseInLocation
    // parses the time in given location, if the
    // string does not contain time zone definition
    t, err = time.ParseInLocation("2/1/2006 3:04 PM ",
                  "31/7/2015 1:25 AM ", time.Local)
    if err != nil {
      panic(err)
    }
    fmt.Println(t)

  }
```

4. Execute the code by running `go run parse.go` in the main Terminal.
5. You will see the following output:

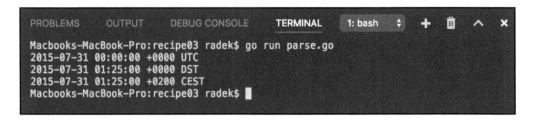

How it works...

The time package contains the Parse function for parsing the string with time information.

The format of an incoming date string is given by the referential date, formatted to the matching format. Remember that the reference time is Jan 2 15:04:05 2006 MST.

If the given time string does not contain the information about the timezone, the result of the Parse function will always be in UTC.

If the timezone information is provided, then the time is always the time instant in the provided timezone.

The ParseInLocation function accepts the third argument, which is the location. If the time string does not contain any timezone information, then the time is parsed to the Time instance in given location.

Converting dates to epoch and vice versa

The epoch is the universal system to describe the point in time. The beginning of epoch time is defined as 00:00:00 1 Jan 1970 UTC. The value of epoch is the amount of seconds since the timestamp, minus the amount of leap seconds since then.

The time package and Time type provide you with the ability to operate and find out the UNIX epoch time.

How to do it...

1. Open the console and create the folder chapter04/recipe04.
2. Navigate to the directory.
3. Create the epoch.go file with the following content:

```
package main

import (
  "fmt"
  "time"
)

func main() {
```

```
// Set the epoch from int64
t := time.Unix(0, 0)
fmt.Println(t)

// Get the epoch
// from Time instance
epoch := t.Unix()
fmt.Println(epoch)

// Current epoch time
apochNow := time.Now().Unix()
fmt.Printf("Epoch time in seconds: %d\n", apochNow)

apochNano := time.Now().UnixNano()
fmt.Printf("Epoch time in nano-seconds: %d\n", apochNano)

}
```

4. Execute the code by running `go run epoch.go` in the main Terminal.
5. You will see the following output:

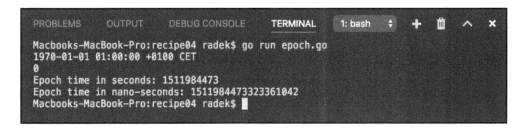

How it works...

The `time` package contains the `Unix` function which accepts two `int64` arguments, and the seconds and nanoseconds of epoch time. This way, you can get the `Time` instance from the epoch value.

To obtain the epoch value from the `Time` instance, the method with the same name as the creation of `Time` from epoch, `Unix`, can be called. There is one more method called `UnixNano`, which returns the count of milliseconds instead of seconds.

Retrieving time units from the date

The `Time` type also provides the API to retrieve time units from the instance. This means you are able to find out what day in a month or what hour in a day the instance represents. This recipe shows how to obtain such units.

How to do it...

1. Open the console and create the folder `chapter04/recipe05`.
2. Navigate to the directory.
3. Create the `units.go` file with the following content:

```go
package main

import (
  "fmt"
  "time"
)

func main() {
    t := time.Date(2017, 11, 29, 21, 0, 0, 0, time.Local)
    fmt.Printf("Extracting units from: %v\n", t)

    dOfMonth := t.Day()
    weekDay := t.Weekday()
    month := t.Month()

    fmt.Printf("The %dth day of %v is %v\n", dOfMonth,
            month, weekDay)

}
```

4. Execute the code by running `go run units.go` in the main Terminal.
5. You will see the following output:

```
PROBLEMS    OUTPUT    DEBUG CONSOLE    TERMINAL    1: bash

Macbooks-MacBook-Pro:recipe05 radek$ go run units.go
Extracting units from: 2017-11-29 21:00:00 +0100 CET
The 29th day of November is Wednesday
Macbooks-MacBook-Pro:recipe05 radek$
```

How it works...

The `Time` type provides methods to extract time units. The preceding example shows the extraction of a weekday, month, and the day of a month. Similarly, the hour, seconds, and other units can be extracted.

Naturally, the units that are not provided by the API directly need to be derived from the existing one.

Date arithmetics

The `Time` type of the `time` package also allows you to perform basic arithmetic on the given date and time. This way, you can find out past and future dates.

How to do it...

1. Open the console and create the folder `chapter04/recipe06`.
2. Navigate to the directory.
3. Create the `arithmetics.go` file with the following content:

```
package main

import (
  "fmt"
  "time"
)

func main() {

  l, err := time.LoadLocation("Europe/Vienna")
  if err != nil {
    panic(err)
  }
  t := time.Date(2017, 11, 30, 11, 10, 20, 0, l)
  fmt.Printf("Default date is: %v\n", t)

  // Add 3 days
  r1 := t.Add(72 * time.Hour)
  fmt.Printf("Default date +3HRS is: %v\n", r1)

  // Subtract 3 days
```

```
r1 = t.Add(-72 * time.Hour)
fmt.Printf("Default date -3HRS is: %v\n", r1)

// More comfortable api
// to add days/months/years
r1 = t.AddDate(1, 3, 2)
fmt.Printf("Default date +1YR +3MTH +2D is: %v\n", r1)

}
```

4. Execute the code by running `go run arithmetics.go` in the main Terminal.
5. You will see the following output:

How it works...

The `Time` type of the `time` package provides two essential methods to operate on date and time.

The first method, `Add`, accepts the `time.Duration` and `AddDate`. With the `Add` method, you can shift the time toward the future with the positive sign and move the time backward just by adding the negative sign.

The second method, `AddDate`, consumes the `int64` arguments as the year, month, and day, and adds the bigger time amounts.

Beware that `AddDate` normalizes the result, the same as the `time.Date` function. Normalization means that adding the month to Aug-31 will result in Oct-1, because the following month contains only 30 days (Sep-31 does not exist).

Finding the difference between two dates

Finding the difference between two dates is not an unusual task. For this operation, the Go standard package time, respectively the Time type, provides supporting methods.

How to do it...

1. Open the console and create the folder chapter04/recipe07.
2. Navigate to the directory.
3. Create the diff.go file with the following content:

```go
package main

import (
  "fmt"
  "time"
)

func main() {

  l, err := time.LoadLocation("Europe/Vienna")
  if err != nil {
    panic(err)
  }
  t := time.Date(2000, 1, 1, 0, 0, 0, 0, l)
  t2 := time.Date(2000, 1, 3, 0, 0, 0, 0, l)
  fmt.Printf("First Default date is %v\n", t)
  fmt.Printf("Second Default date is %v\n", t2)

  dur := t2.Sub(t)
  fmt.Printf("The duration between t and t2 is %v\n", dur)

  dur = time.Since(t)
  fmt.Printf("The duration between now and t is %v\n", dur)

  dur = time.Until(t)
  fmt.Printf("The duration between t and now is %v\n", dur)

}
```

4. Execute the code by running `go run diff.go` in the main Terminal.

5. You will see the following output:

How it works...

The `Sub` method of the `Time` instance is the universal one to find out the difference between two dates. The result is `time.Duration`, which represents the nanosecond count between these dates.

Note that if the difference exceeds the limit of the maximum/minimum `time.Duration`, then the maximum or minimum is returned.

The functions `Since` and `Until` are just a shorter way on how to work out the difference between now and the given date. These work as their names prompts. The `Since` function returns the same result as `time.Now().Sub(t)`; similarly, the `Until` returns the same result as `t.Sub(time.Now())`.

The `Sub` method naturally also counts with time zones. So, the difference is returned with respect to the location of each `Time` instance.

Converting between time zones

Dealing with time zones is hard. A good way to handle the different time zones is to keep one timezone as referential in the system and convert the others if needed. This recipe shows you how the conversion of time between time zones is done.

How to do it...

1. Open the console and create the folder `chapter04/recipe08`.
2. Navigate to the directory.
3. Create the `timezones.go` file with the following content:

```go
package main

import (
  "fmt"
  "time"
)

func main() {
  eur, err := time.LoadLocation("Europe/Vienna")
  if err != nil {
    panic(err)
  }

  t := time.Date(2000, 1, 1, 0, 0, 0, 0, eur)
  fmt.Printf("Original Time: %v\n", t)

  phx, err := time.LoadLocation("America/Phoenix")
  if err != nil {
    panic(err)
  }

  t2 := t.In(phx)
  fmt.Printf("Converted Time: %v\n", t2)

}
```

4. Execute the code by running `go run timezones.go` in the main Terminal.
5. You will see the following output:

```
PROBLEMS    OUTPUT    DEBUG CONSOLE    TERMINAL    1: bash  ⬍  +  🗑  ∧  ✕
Macbooks-MacBook-Pro:recipe08 radek$  go run timezones.go
Original Time: 2000-01-01 00:00:00 +0100 CET
Converted Time: 1999-12-31 16:00:00 -0700 MST
Macbooks-MacBook-Pro:recipe08 radek$ ▊
```

How it works...

The `Time` type provides the `In` method which consumes the pointer to `time.Location`. The returned `Time` is the original one converted to the given time zone. Note that the `Time` instance is considered to be immutable, so the methods changing the instance result in a new `Time` instance.

The `time` package refers to the *IANA Time Zone* database as a source of locations. The `LoadLocation` function looks for the directory or ZIP file from the `ZONEINFO` environment variable. If not found, the known installation locations on UNIX systems are searched. Finally, it looks in `$GOROOT/lib/time/zoneinfo.zip`.

Running the code block periodically

Besides the date and time operations, the `time` package also provides support for periodic and delayed code execution. Typically, the application health checks, activity checks, or any periodic job can be implemented this way.

How to do it...

1. Open the console and create the folder `chapter04/recipe09`.
2. Navigate to the directory.
3. Create the `ticker.go` file with the following content:

```
package main

import (
  "fmt"
  "os"
  "os/signal"
  "time"
)

func main() {

  c := make(chan os.Signal, 1)
  signal.Notify(c)

  ticker := time.NewTicker(time.Second)
```

```go
        stop := make(chan bool)

        go func() {
          defer func() { stop <- true }()
          for {
            select {
              case <-ticker.C:
                fmt.Println("Tick")
              case <-stop:
                fmt.Println("Goroutine closing")
                return
            }
          }
        }()

        // Block until
        // the signal is received
        <-c
        ticker.Stop()

        // Stop the goroutine
        stop <- true
        // Wait until the
        <-stop
        fmt.Println("Application stopped")
    }
```

4. Execute the code by running `go run ticker.go` in the main Terminal.
5. Wait a few seconds, and then press *Ctrl* + *C* to send `SIGINT` a signal.
6. You will see the following output:

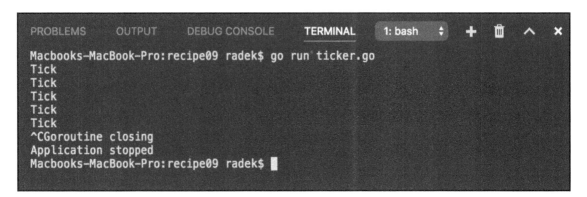

How it works...

The `Ticker` holds the `C` channel which delivers the periodical ticks. The instance is created with a given interval between ticks. The interval is defined by the `time.Duration` value.

The code which is intended to be executed periodically is executed in the goroutine in an infinite loop. The reading from the `Ticker` channel blocks the loop until the tick is delivered.

Note that once the `Ticker` is stopped by calling the `Stop` method, the `C` channel is not closed, it just stops delivering the ticks. For this reason, the preceding code contains the `select` construct where the stop channel can deliver the stop signal. This way, a graceful shutdown can be done.

Waiting a certain amount of time

The previous recipe describes how to execute the code periodically. This recipe will show you how to execute the code with a delay.

How to do it...

1. Open the console and create the folder `chapter04/recipe10`.
2. Navigate to the directory.
3. Create the `delay.go` file with the following content:

```
package main

import (
  "fmt"
  "sync"
  "time"
)

func main() {

  t := time.NewTimer(3 * time.Second)

  fmt.Printf("Start waiting at %v\n",
            time.Now().Format(time.UnixDate))
  <-t.C
```

```
        fmt.Printf("Code executed at %v\n",
                time.Now().Format(time.UnixDate))

    wg := &sync.WaitGroup{}
    wg.Add(1)
    fmt.Printf("Start waiting for AfterFunc at %v\n",
                time.Now().Format(time.UnixDate))
    time.AfterFunc(3*time.Second, func() {
    fmt.Printf("Code executed for AfterFunc at %v\n",
                time.Now().Format(time.UnixDate))
        wg.Done()
    })

    wg.Wait()

    fmt.Printf("Waiting on time.After at %v\n",
                time.Now().Format(time.UnixDate))
    <-time.After(3 * time.Second)
    fmt.Printf("Code resumed at %v\n",
                time.Now().Format(time.UnixDate))

    }
```

4. Execute the code by running go run delay.go in the main Terminal.
5. You will see the following output:

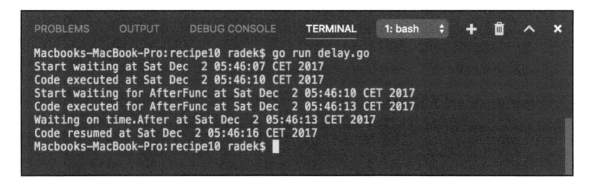

How it works...

To execute the code with some delay only once, the Timer from the time package can be used. The concept of how this works is the same as described in the previous recipe, *Running the code block periodically*.

The `Timer` contains the `C` channel, which delivers the tick after a given time. After that, no other ticks are delivered through the channel.

The same functionality delivers the `AfterFunc` function of the `time` package. It just simplifies the usage. Note that there is no channel needed. The sample code uses the `sync.WaitGroup` to wait until the given function is executed.

The `time.After` is the last option in the preceding example. The function returns a channel that delivers the tick after a given period. Note the difference between the `Timer` and `After` functions. The `Timer` is the reusable structure (it provides the `Stop` and `Reset` methods). On the other hand, the `After` function can only be used once as it does not provide any reset option.

Timeout long-running operations

The previous recipe describes the concept of executing the code with some delay. The same concept can be used to implement the timeout for long running operations. This recipe will illustrate how this can be done.

How to do it...

1. Open the console and create the folder `chapter04/recipe11`.
2. Navigate to the directory.
3. Create the `timeout.go` file with the following content:

```go
package main

import (
  "fmt"
  "time"
)

func main() {

    to := time.After(3 * time.Second)
    list := make([]string, 0)
    done := make(chan bool, 1)

    fmt.Println("Starting to insert items")
    go func() {
```

```
        defer fmt.Println("Exiting goroutine")
        for {
          select {
            case <-to:
              fmt.Println("The time is up")
              done <- true
              return
            default:
              list = append(list, time.Now().String())
          }
        }
      }()

      <-done
      fmt.Printf("Managed to insert %d items\n", len(list))
    }
```

4. Execute the code by running `go run timeout.go` in the main Terminal.
5. You will see the following output:

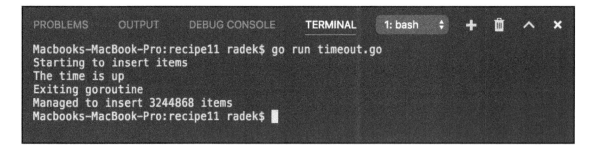

How it works...

The timeout for the long-running operation in the previous code is implemented with the use of the `time.After` function, which provides the channel delivering the tick after the given period.

The operation itself is wrapped to select a statement which chooses between the `time.After` channel and the default option, which executes the operation.

Note that you need to allow the code to read from the `time.After` channel periodically to find out whether the timeout is exceeded or not. Otherwise, if the default code branch blocks the execution entirely, there is no way how to find out if the timeout has already elapsed.

There's more...

The example implementation uses the `time.After` function, but the `Timer` function can also be used in the same way. The built-in libraries also use the `context.WithTimeout` to implement timeout functionality.

Serializing the time and date

When serializing the date and time information, it is necessary to choose the proper format. This recipe will illustrate how the `time` package helps to choose one and do the serialization properly.

How to do it...

1. Open the console and create the folder `chapter04/recipe12`.
2. Navigate to the directory.
3. Create the `serialize.go` file with the following content:

```go
package main

import (
    "encoding/json"
    "fmt"
    "time"
)

func main() {

    eur, err := time.LoadLocation("Europe/Vienna")
    if err != nil {
        panic(err)
    }
    t := time.Date(2017, 11, 20, 11, 20, 10, 0, eur)

    // json.Marshaler interface
    b, err := t.MarshalJSON()
    if err != nil {
        panic(err)
    }
    fmt.Println("Serialized as RFC 3339:", string(b))
```

```go
    t2 := time.Time{}
    t2.UnmarshalJSON(b)
    fmt.Println("Deserialized from RFC 3339:", t2)

    // Serialize as epoch
    epoch := t.Unix()
    fmt.Println("Serialized as Epoch:", epoch)

    // Deserialize epoch
    jsonStr := fmt.Sprintf("{ \"created\":%d }", epoch)
    data := struct {
      Created int64 `json:"created"`
    }{}
    json.Unmarshal([]byte(jsonStr), &data)
    deserialized := time.Unix(data.Created, 0)
    fmt.Println("Deserialized from Epoch:", deserialized)

}
```

4. Execute the code by running `go run serialize.go` in the main Terminal.
5. You will see the following output:

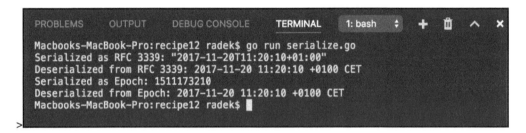

How it works...

The `Time` function implements the interfaces for Binary, Gob, and JSON serialization. The JSON format is considered to be very universal, so an example on how the value is serialized to JSON is shown. Note that the `Time` function serializes the value in the manner of RFC 3339 (https://www.ietf.org/rfc/rfc3339.txt), which proposes a so-called internet date/time format.

Another very universal way to serialize/keep the time is to use the epoch time. The epoch time is independent of timezones because it is defined by seconds/nanoseconds elapsed since an absolute point in time. Finally, it is represented as a number so there is no reason to serialize and deserialize the value.

5
In and Out

This chapter contains the following recipes:

- Reading standard input
- Writing standard output and error
- Opening a file by name
- Reading the file into a string
- Reading/writing a different charset
- Seeking a position within a file
- Reading and writing binary data
- Writing to multiple writers at once
- Piping between writer and reader
- Serializing objects to binary format
- Reading and writing ZIP files
- Parsing a large XML file effectively
- Extracting data from an incomplete JSON array

Introduction

This chapter will go through typical I/O operations and related tasks, as well as the writing and reading of various input sources. We will go through XML processing, unzipping compressed files, and using the random access file.

Check if Go is properly installed. The *Getting ready* section from *Retrieving the Golang version* recipe of Chapter 1, *Interacting with the Environment*, will help you.

Reading standard input

Every process owns its standard input, output, and error file descriptor. The stdin serves as the input of the process. This recipe describes how to read the data from the stdin.

How to do it...

1. Open the console and create the folder chapter05/recipe01.
2. Navigate to the directory.
3. Create the fmt.go file with the following content:

```go
package main

import (
  "fmt"
)

func main() {

  var name string
  fmt.Println("What is your name?")
  fmt.Scanf("%s\n", &name)

  var age int
  fmt.Println("What is your age?")
  fmt.Scanf("%d\n", &age)

  fmt.Printf("Hello %s, your age is %d\n", name, age)

}
```

4. Execute the code with go run fmt.go.
5. Enter the input John and press *Enter*.
6. Enter the input 40 and press *Enter*.

7. You will see the following output:

```
PROBLEMS    OUTPUT    DEBUG CONSOLE    TERMINAL    1: bash ⇕    ✚    🗑    ∧    ✕
Macbooks-MacBook-Pro:recipe01 radek$ go run fmt.go
What is your name?
John
What is your age?
40
Hello John, your age is 40
Macbooks-MacBook-Pro:recipe01 radek$ []
```

8. Create the file `scanner.go` with the following content:

```go
package main

import (
   "bufio"
   "fmt"
   "os"
)

func main() {

   // The Scanner is able to
   // scan input by lines
   sc := bufio.NewScanner(os.Stdin)

   for sc.Scan() {
     txt := sc.Text()
     fmt.Printf("Echo: %s\n", txt)
   }

}
```

9. Execute the code with `go run scanner.go`.
10. Enter the input `Hello` and press *Enter*.
11. Press *CTRL + C* to send `SIGINT`.

12. See the output:

```
PROBLEMS    OUTPUT    DEBUG CONSOLE    TERMINAL    1: go  ⬍    +  🗑  ∧  ✕
Macbooks-MacBook-Pro:recipe01 radek$ go run scanner.go
Hello
Echo: Hello
▌
```

13. Create the file `reader.go` with the following content:

```go
package main

import (
  "fmt"
  "os"
)

func main() {

  for {
    data := make([]byte, 8)
    n, err := os.Stdin.Read(data)
    if err == nil && n > 0 {
      process(data)
    } else {
      break
    }
  }

}

func process(data []byte) {
  fmt.Printf("Received: %X %s\n", data, string(data))
}
```

14. Execute the code with the piped input `echo 'Go is awesome!' | go run reader.go`.

15. See the output:

```
PROBLEMS    OUTPUT    DEBUG CONSOLE    TERMINAL    1: bash ‚ô¥   +  üóë  ^  ‚úñ

Macbooks-MacBook-Pro:recipe01 radek$ echo 'Go is awesome!' | go run reader.go
Received: 476F206973206177        Go is aw
Received: 65736F6D65210A00        esome!

Macbooks-MacBook-Pro:recipe01 radek$ ‚ñà
```

How it works...

The `stdin` of the Go process could be retrieved via the `Stdin` of the `os` package. In fact, it is a `File` type which implements the `Reader` interface. Reading from the `Reader` is then very easy. The preceding code shows three very common ways of how to read from the `Stdin`.

The first option illustrates the use of the `fmt` package, which provides the functions `Scan`, `Scanf`, and `Scanln`. The `Scanf` function reads the input into given variable(s). The advantage of `Scanf` is that you can determine the format of the scanned value. The `Scan` function just reads the input into a variable (without predefined formatting) and `Scanln`, as its name suggests, reads the input ended with the line break.

The `Scanner`, which is the second option shown in the sample code, provides a convenient way of scanning larger input. The `Scanner` contains the function `Split` by which the custom split function could be defined. For example, to scan the words from `stdin`, you can use `bufio.ScanWords` predefined `SplitFunc`.

The reading via the `Reader` API is the last presented approach. This one provides you with more control of how the input is read.

Writing standard output and error

As the previous recipe describes, each process has `stdin`, a `stdout` and `stderr` file descriptors. The standard approach is the use of `stdout` as a process output and `stderr` as process error output. As these are the file descriptors, the destination where the data is written could be anything, from the console to the socket. This recipe will show you how to write the `stdout` and `stderr`.

How to do it...

1. Open the console and create the folder chapter05/recipe02.
2. Navigate to the directory.
3. Create the stdouterr.go file with the following content:

```
package main

import (
  "fmt"
  "io"
  "os"
 )

func main() {

  // Simply write string
  io.WriteString(os.Stdout,
  "This is string to standard output.\n")

  io.WriteString(os.Stderr,
  "This is string to standard error output.\n")

  // Stdout/err implements
  // writer interface
  buf := []byte{0xAF, 0xFF, 0xFE}
  for i := 0; i < 200; i++ {
    if _, e := os.Stdout.Write(buf); e != nil {
      panic(e)
    }
  }

  // The fmt package
  // could be used too
  fmt.Fprintln(os.Stdout, "\n")
}
```

4. Execute the code with go run stdouterr.go.

5. See the output:

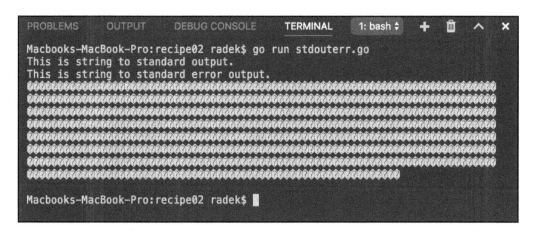

How it works...

As with the `Stdin` from the previous recipe, the `Stdout` and `Stderr` are the file descriptors. So these are implementing the `Writer` interface.

The preceding example shows a few ways of how to write into these via the `io.WriteString` function, with the use of the `Writer` API and by the `fmt` package and `FprintXX` functions.

Opening a file by name

File access is a very common operation used to store or read the data. This recipe illustrates how to open a file by its name and path, using the standard library.

How to do it...

1. Open the console and create the folder `chapter05/recipe03`.
2. Navigate to the directory.
3. Create the directory `temp` and create the file `file.txt` in it.

4. Edit the `file.txt` file and write `This file content` into the file.
5. Create the `openfile.go` file with the following content:

```
package main

import (
  "fmt"
  "io"
  "io/ioutil"
  "os"
)

func main() {

  f, err := os.Open("temp/file.txt")
  if err != nil {
    panic(err)
  }

  c, err := ioutil.ReadAll(f)
  if err != nil {
    panic(err)
  }

  fmt.Printf("### File content ###\n%s\n", string(c))
  f.Close()

  f, err = os.OpenFile("temp/test.txt", os.O_CREATE|os.O_RDWR,
                    os.ModePerm)
  if err != nil {
    panic(err)
  }
  io.WriteString(f, "Test string")
  f.Close()

}
```

6. The file structure should look like this:

7. Execute the code with `go run openfile.go`.
8. See the output there should also be a new file, `test.txt`, in the `temp` folder:

How it works...

The `os` package offers a simple way of opening the file. The function `Open` opens the file by the path, just in read-only mode. Another function, `OpenFile,` is the more powerful one and consumes the path to the file, flags, and permissions.

The flag constants are defined in the `os` package and you can combine them with use of the binary OR operator `|`. The permissions are set by the `os` package constants (for example, `os.ModePerm`) or by the number notation such as `0777` (permissions: `-rwxrwxrwx`).

Reading the file into a string

In the previous recipes, we saw the reading from `Stdin` and the opening of the file. In this recipe, we will combine these two a little bit and show how to read the file into a string.

How to do it...

1. Open the console and create the folder `chapter05/recipe04`.
2. Navigate to the directory.
3. Create the directory `temp` and create the file `file.txt` in it.
4. Edit the `file.txt` file and write multiple lines into the file.

5. Create the `readfile.go` file with the following content:

```go
package main

import "os"
import "bufio"

import "bytes"
import "fmt"
import "io/ioutil"

func main() {

  fmt.Println("### Read as reader ###")
  f, err := os.Open("temp/file.txt")
  if err != nil {
    panic(err)
  }
  defer f.Close()

  // Read the
  // file with reader
  wr := bytes.Buffer{}
  sc := bufio.NewScanner(f)
  for sc.Scan() {
    wr.WriteString(sc.Text())
  }
  fmt.Println(wr.String())

  fmt.Println("### ReadFile ###")
  // for smaller files
  fContent, err := ioutil.ReadFile("temp/file.txt")
  if err != nil {
    panic(err)
  }
  fmt.Println(string(fContent))

}
```

6. Execute the code with `go run readfile.go`.
7. See the output:

```
PROBLEMS    OUTPUT    DEBUG CONSOLE    TERMINAL    1: bash ⬍    +  🗑  ∧  ✕
Macbooks-MacBook-Pro:recipe04 radek$ go run readfile.go
### Read as reader ###
Lorem ipsum dolor sit amet, consectetur adipiscing elit. Mauris id pretium er
os. Aliquam imperdiet mi ut elit faucibus porta. Donec facilisis nunc at risu
s dapibus elementum.
### ReadFile ###
Lorem ipsum dolor sit amet, consectetur adipiscing elit.
Mauris id pretium eros. Aliquam imperdiet mi ut elit faucibus porta.
Donec facilisis nunc at risus dapibus elementum.
Macbooks-MacBook-Pro:recipe04 radek$ ▌
```

How it works...

The reading from the file is simple because the `File` type implements both the `Reader` and `Writer` interfaces. This way, all functions and approaches applicable to the `Reader` interface are applicable to the `File` type. The preceding example shows how to read the file with the use of `Scanner` and write the content to the bytes buffer (which is more performant than string concatenation). This way, you are able to control the volume of content read from a file.

The second approach with `ioutil.ReadFile` is simpler but should be used carefully, because it reads the whole file. Keep in mind that the file could be huge and it could threaten the stability of the application.

Reading/writing a different charset

It is not an exception that the input from various sources could come in various charsets. Note that a lot of systems use the Windows operating system but there are others. Go, by default, expects that the strings used in the program are UTF-8 based. If they are not, then decoding from the given charset must be done to be able to work with the string. This recipe will show the reading and writing of the file in a charset other than UTF-8.

How to do it...

1. Open the console and create the folder `chapter05/recipe05`.
2. Navigate to the directory.
3. Create the `charset.go` file with the following content:

```
package main

import (
  "fmt"
  "io/ioutil"
  "os"

  "golang.org/x/text/encoding/charmap"
)

func main() {

  // Write the string
  // encoded to Windows-1252
  encoder := charmap.Windows1252.NewEncoder()
  s, e := encoder.String("This is sample text with runs Š")
  if e != nil {
    panic(e)
  }
  ioutil.WriteFile("example.txt", []byte(s), os.ModePerm)

  // Decode to UTF-8
  f, e := os.Open("example.txt")
  if e != nil {
    panic(e)
  }
  defer f.Close()
  decoder := charmap.Windows1252.NewDecoder()
  reader := decoder.Reader(f)
  b, err := ioutil.ReadAll(reader)
  if err != nil {
    panic(err)
  }
  fmt.Println(string(b))
}
```

4. Execute the code with `go run charset.go`.

5. See the output:

```
PROBLEMS   OUTPUT   DEBUG CONSOLE   TERMINAL   1: bash ↕   +  🗑  ∧  ✕

Macbooks-MacBook-Pro:recipe05 radek$ go run charset.go
This is sample text with runes Š
Macbooks-MacBook-Pro:recipe05 radek$ ▊
```

How it works...

The `golang.org/x/text/encoding/charmap` package contains the `Charmap` type pointer constants that represent the widely used charsets. The `Charmap` type provides the methods for creating the encoder and decoder for the given charset. The `Encoder` creates the encoding `Writer` which encodes the written bytes into the chosen charset. Similarly, the `Decoder` can create the decoding `Reader`, which decodes all read data from the chosen charset.

See also

`Chapter 2`, *String and Things,* also contains the recipe *Decoding a string from the non-Unicode charset* for encoding/decoding a string into another charset.

Seeking a position within a file

In some cases, you need to read from or write to a particular location in a file, such as an indexed file. The recipe will show you how to use the position seeking in the context of flat file operations.

How to do it...

1. Open the console and create the folder `chapter05/recipe06`.
2. Navigate to the directory.

3. Create the file `flatfile.txt` with the following content:

```
123.Jun.......Wong......
12..Novak.....Jurgen....
10..Thomas....Sohlich...
```

4. Create the `fileseek.go` file with the following content:

```go
package main

import (
  "errors"
  "fmt"
  "os"
)

const lineLegth = 25

func main() {

    f, e := os.OpenFile("flatfile.txt", os.O_RDWR|os.O_CREATE,
                        os.ModePerm)
    if e != nil {
      panic(e)
    }
    defer f.Close()

    fmt.Println(readRecords(2, "last", f))
    if err := writeRecord(2, "first", "Radomir", f); err != nil {
      panic(err)
    }
    fmt.Println(readRecords(2, "first", f))
    if err := writeRecord(10, "first", "Andrew", f); err != nil {
      panic(err)
    }
    fmt.Println(readRecords(10, "first", f))
    fmt.Println(readLine(2, f))
}

func readLine(line int, f *os.File) (string, error) {
  lineBuffer := make([]byte, 24)
  f.Seek(int64(line*lineLegth), 0)
  _, err := f.Read(lineBuffer)
  return string(lineBuffer), err
}

func writeRecord(line int, column, dataStr string, f *os.File)
```

```
error {
  definedLen := 10
  position := int64(line * lineLegth)
  switch column {
    case "id":
      definedLen = 4
    case "first":
      position += 4
    case "last":
      position += 14
   default:
      return errors.New("Column not defined")
  }

  if len([]byte(dataStr)) > definedLen {
    return fmt.Errorf("Maximum length for '%s' is %d",
                      column, definedLen)
  }

  data := make([]byte, definedLen)
  for i := range data {
    data[i] = '.'
  }
  copy(data, []byte(dataStr))
  _, err := f.WriteAt(data, position)
  return err
}

func readRecords(line int, column string, f *os.File)
               (string, error) {
  lineBuffer := make([]byte, 24)
  f.ReadAt(lineBuffer, int64(line*lineLegth))
  var retVal string
  switch column {
    case "id":
      return string(lineBuffer[:3]), nil
    case "first":
      return string(lineBuffer[4:13]), nil
    case "last":
      return string(lineBuffer[14:23]), nil
  }

  return retVal, errors.New("Column not defined")
}
```

5. Execute the code with `go run fileseek.go`.

6. See the output:

```
PROBLEMS    OUTPUT    DEBUG CONSOLE    TERMINAL    1: bash ÷    +   🗑  ∧   ✕

Macbooks-MacBook-Pro:recipe06 radek$ go run fileseek.go
Sohlich.. <nil>
Radomir.. <nil>
Andrew... <nil>
10..Radomir...Sohlich... <nil>
Macbooks-MacBook-Pro:recipe06 radek$ []
```

7. Display the file in hex `xxd flatfile.txt`.

```
PROBLEMS    OUTPUT    DEBUG CONSOLE    TERMINAL    1: bash ÷    +   🗑  ∧   ✕

Macbooks-MacBook-Pro:recipe06 radek$ xxd flatfile.txt
00000000: 3132 332e 4a75 6e2e 2e2e 2e2e 2e2e 576f   123.Jun.......Wo
00000010: 6e67 2e2e 2e2e 2e2e 0a31 322e 2e4e 6f76   ng.......12..Nov
00000020: 616b 2e2e 2e2e 2e4a 7572 6765 6e2e 2e2e   ak.....Jurgen...
00000030: 2e0a 3130 2e2e 5261 646f 6d69 722e 2e2e   ..10..Radomir...
00000040: 536f 686c 6963 682e 2e2e 0000 0000 0000   Sohlich.........
00000050: 0000 0000 0000 0000 0000 0000 0000 0000   ................
00000060: 0000 0000 0000 0000 0000 0000 0000 0000   ................
00000070: 0000 0000 0000 0000 0000 0000 0000 0000   ................
00000080: 0000 0000 0000 0000 0000 0000 0000 0000   ................
00000090: 0000 0000 0000 0000 0000 0000 0000 0000   ................
000000a0: 0000 0000 0000 0000 0000 0000 0000 0000   ................
000000b0: 0000 0000 0000 0000 0000 0000 0000 0000   ................
000000c0: 0000 0000 0000 0000 0000 0000 0000 0000   ................
000000d0: 0000 0000 0000 0000 0000 0000 0000 0000   ................
000000e0: 0000 0000 0000 0000 0000 0000 0000 0000   ................
000000f0: 0000 0000 0000 0000 0000 0000 0000 416e   ..............An
00000100: 6472 6577 2e2e 2e2e                        drew....
Macbooks-MacBook-Pro:recipe06 radek$ |
```

How it works...

The preceding example uses the `flatfile` as an illustration of how to seek, read and write at the position in the file. In general, for moving the position of the current pointer in the `File`, the `Seek` method can be used. It takes two arguments and these are, position and how to count the position, `0 - relative to file origin`, `1 - relative to current position`, `2 - relative to the end of file`. This way you are able to move the cursor within the file. The `Seek` method is used in the implementation of the `readLine` function in the preceding code.

The flatfile is the most basic form of how to store the data. The record structure has a fixed length and the same for the record parts. The structure of the flat file in the example is: ID - 4 chars, FirstName - 10 chars, LastName - 10 chars. The whole record is 24 chars long, ended by a line break which is the 25th character.

The os.File also contains the ReadAt and WriteAt methods. These methods consume that the bytes to be written/read and the offset where to start. These simplify the writing and reading to a certain position in a file.

 Note that the example assumes that each rune is only one byte, which does not have to be true for special characters, and so on.

Reading and writing binary data

This recipe describes how to write and read any type in the binary form.

How to do it...

1. Open the console and create the folder chapter05/recipe07.
2. Navigate to the directory.
3. Create the rwbinary.go file with the following content:

```
package main

import (
  "bytes"
  "encoding/binary"
  "fmt"
)

func main() {
  // Writing binary values
  buf := bytes.NewBuffer([]byte{})
  if err := binary.Write(buf, binary.BigEndian, 1.004);
  err != nil {
    panic(err)
  }
```

```
    if err := binary.Write(buf, binary.BigEndian,
            []byte("Hello")); err != nil {
      panic(err)
    }

    // Reading the written values
    var num float64
    if err := binary.Read(buf, binary.BigEndian, &num);
    err != nil {
      panic(err)
    }
    fmt.Printf("float64: %.3f\n", num)
    greeting := make([]byte, 5)
    if err := binary.Read(buf, binary.BigEndian, &greeting);
    err != nil {
      panic(err)
    }
    fmt.Printf("string: %s\n", string(greeting))
}
```

4. Execute the code by `go run rwbinary.go`.
5. See the output:

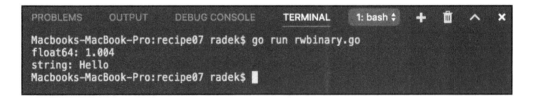

How it works...

The binary data could be written with the use of the `encoding/binary` package. The function `Write` consumes the `Writer` where the data should be written, the byte order (`BigEndian`/`LittleEndian`) and finally, the value to be written into `Writer`.

To read the binary data analogically, the `Read` function could be used. Note that there is no magic in reading the data from the binary source. You need to be sure what data you are fetching from the `Reader`. If not, the data could be fetched into any type which fits the size.

Writing to multiple writers at once

When you need to write the same output into more than one target, there is a helping hand available in the built-in package. This recipe shows how to implement writing simultaneously into multiple targets.

How to do it...

1. Open the console and create the folder `chapter05/recipe08`.
2. Navigate to the directory.
3. Create the `multiwr.go` file with the following content:

```
package main

import "io"
import "bytes"
import "os"
import "fmt"

func main() {

  buf := bytes.NewBuffer([]byte{})
  f, err := os.OpenFile("sample.txt", os.O_CREATE|os.O_RDWR,
                        os.ModePerm)
  if err != nil {
    panic(err)
  }
  wr := io.MultiWriter(buf, f)
  _, err = io.WriteString(wr, "Hello, Go is awesome!")
  if err != nil {
    panic(err)
  }

  fmt.Println("Content of buffer: " + buf.String())
}
```

4. Execute the code by `go run multiwr.go`.

5. See the output:

```
PROBLEMS    OUTPUT    DEBUG CONSOLE    TERMINAL    1: bash ⇕    +    🗑    ⌃    ✕
Macbooks-MacBook-Pro:recipe08 radek$ go run multiwr.go
Content of buffer: Hello, Go is awesome!
Macbooks-MacBook-Pro:recipe08 radek$ ▉
```

6. Check the content of the created file:

```
Hello, Go is awesome!
```

How it works...

The io package contains the MultiWriter function with variadic parameters of Writers.
When the Write method on the Writer is called, then the data is written to all underlying
Writers.

Piping between writer and reader

The pipes between processes are the easy way to use the output of the first process as the
input of other processes. The same concept could be done in Go, for example, to pipe data
from one socket to another socket, to create the tunneled connection. This recipe will show
you how to create the pipe with use of the Go built-in library.

How to do it...

1. Open the console and create the folder chapter05/recipe09.
2. Navigate to the directory.
3. Create the pipe.go file with the following content:

```
package main

import (
  "io"
  "log"
  "os"
  "os/exec"
```

```
)

func main() {
  pReader, pWriter := io.Pipe()

  cmd := exec.Command("echo", "Hello Go!\nThis is example")
  cmd.Stdout = pWriter

  go func() {
    defer pReader.Close()
    if _, err := io.Copy(os.Stdout, pReader); err != nil {
      log.Fatal(err)
    }
  }()

  if err := cmd.Run(); err != nil {
    log.Fatal(err)
  }

}
```

4. Execute the code by `go run pipe.go`.

5. See the output:

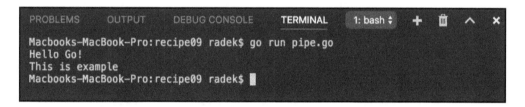

How it works...

The `io.Pipe` function creates the in-memory pipe and returns both ends of the pipe, the `PipeReader` on one side and `PipeWriter` on the other side. Each `Write` to `PipeWriter` is blocked until it is consumed by `Read` on the other end.

The example shows the piping output from the executed command to the standard output of the parent program. By assigning the `pWriter` to `cmd.Stdout`, the standard output of the child process is written to the pipe, and the `io.Copy` in `goroutine` consumes the written data, by copying the data to `os.Stdout`.

Serializing objects to binary format

Besides the well-known JSON and XML, Go also offers the binary format, gob. This recipe goes through the basic concept of how to use the gob package.

How to do it...

1. Open the console and create the folder chapter05/recipe10.
2. Navigate to the directory.
3. Create the gob.go file with the following content:

```go
package main

import (
  "bytes"
  "encoding/gob"
  "fmt"
)

type User struct {
  FirstName string
  LastName string
  Age int
  Active bool
}

func (u User) String() string {
  return fmt.Sprintf(`{"FirstName":%s,"LastName":%s,
                      "Age":%d,"Active":%v }`,
  u.FirstName, u.LastName, u.Age, u.Active)
}

type SimpleUser struct {
  FirstName string
  LastName string
}

func (u SimpleUser) String() string {
  return fmt.Sprintf(`{"FirstName":%s,"LastName":%s}`,
  u.FirstName, u.LastName)
}

func main() {
```

```
var buff bytes.Buffer

// Encode value
enc := gob.NewEncoder(&buff)
user := User{
  "Radomir",
  "Sohlich",
  30,
  true,
}
enc.Encode(user)
fmt.Printf("%X\n", buff.Bytes())

// Decode value
out := User{}
dec := gob.NewDecoder(&buff)
dec.Decode(&out)
fmt.Println(out.String())

enc.Encode(user)
out2 := SimpleUser{}
dec.Decode(&out2)
fmt.Println(out2.String())

}
```

4. Execute the code by `go run gob.go`.
5. See the output:

```
PROBLEMS    OUTPUT    DEBUG CONSOLE    TERMINAL    1: bash ⇕    ✚  🗑  ∧  ✕

Macbooks-MacBook-Pro:recipe10 radek$ go run gob.go
40FF8103010104557365720 1FF8200010401094669727374 4E616D6501 0C0001084C6173744E6
16D65010C0001034167650104000106416374697665010200000019FF8201075261646F6D6972
0107536F686C696368013C010100
{"FirstName":Radomir,"LastName":Sohlich,"Age":30,"Active":true }
{"FirstName":Radomir,"LastName":Sohlich}
Macbooks-MacBook-Pro:recipe10 radek$ ▮
```

How it works...

The gob serialization and deserialization need the Encoder and Decoder. The gob.NewEncoder function creates the Encoder with the underlying Writer. Each call of the Encode method will serialize the object into a gob format. The gob format itself is the self-describing binary format. This means each serialized struct is preceded by its description.

To decode the data from the serialized form, the Decoder must be created by calling the gob.NewDecoder with the underlying Reader. The Decode then accepts the pointer to the structure where the data should be deserialized.

 Note that the gob format does not need the source and destination type to match exactly. For the rules, refer to the encoding/gob package.

Reading and writing ZIP files

ZIP compression is a widely used compression format. It is usual to use the ZIP format for an application to upload a file set or, on the other hand, export zipped files as output. This recipe will show you how to handle ZIP files programmatically with the use of the standard library.

How to do it...

1. Open the console and create the folder chapter05/recipe11.
2. Navigate to the directory.
3. Create the zip.go file with the following content:

```
package main

import (
  "archive/zip"
  "bytes"
  "fmt"
  "io"
  "io/ioutil"
  "log"
```

```go
    "os"
)

func main() {

  var buff bytes.Buffer

  // Compress content
  zipW := zip.NewWriter(&buff)
  f, err := zipW.Create("newfile.txt")
  if err != nil {
    panic(err)
  }
  _, err = f.Write([]byte("This is my file content"))
  if err != nil {
    panic(err)
  }
  err = zipW.Close()
  if err != nil {
    panic(err)
  }

  //Write output to file
  err = ioutil.WriteFile("data.zip", buff.Bytes(), os.ModePerm)
  if err != nil {
    panic(err)
  }

  // Decompress the content
  zipR, err := zip.OpenReader("data.zip")
  if err != nil {
    panic(err)
  }

  for _, file := range zipR.File {
    fmt.Println("File " + file.Name + " contains:")
    r, err := file.Open()
    if err != nil {
      log.Fatal(err)
    }
    _, err = io.Copy(os.Stdout, r)
    if err != nil {
      panic(err)
    }
    err = r.Close()
    if err != nil {
      panic(err)
    }
```

```
            fmt.Println()
        }

    }
```

4. Execute the code by `go run zip.go`.

5. See the output:

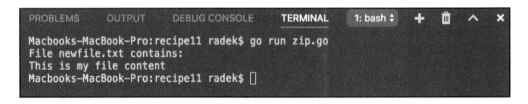

How it works...

The built-in package `zip` contains the `NewWriter` and `NewReader` functions to create the `zip.Writer` to compress, and the `zip.Reader` to decompress the zipped content.

Each record of the ZIP file is created with the `Create` method of the created `zip.Writer`. The returned `Writer` is then used to write the content body.

To decompress the files, the `OpenReader` function is used to create the `ReadCloser` of the records in the zipped file. The `File` field of the created `ReaderCloser` is the slice of `zip.File` pointers. The content of the file is obtained by calling the `Open` method and by reading the returned `ReadCloser`.

> The folders could be created by only adding slashes to the name of the file in the `Create` method. An example could be `folder/newfile.txt`.

Parsing a large XML file effectively

XML is a very common format for data exchange. The Go library contains support for parsing XML files the same way as the JSON. Usually, the struct which corresponds to the XML scheme is used and with this help, the XML content is parsed at once. The problem is when the XML file is too large to fit into memory and so you need to parse the file in chunks. This recipe will reveal how to handle a large XML file and parse the required information.

How to do it...

1. Open the console and create the folder `chapter05/recipe11`.
2. Navigate to the directory.
3. Create the `data.xml` file with the following XML content:

```
<?xml version="1.0"?>
<catalog>
  <book id="bk101">
    <author>Gambardella, Matthew</author>
    <title>XML Developer's Guide</title>
    <genre>Computer</genre>
    <price>44.95</price>
    <publish_date>2000-10-01</publish_date>
    <description>An in-depth look at creating applications
    with XML.</description>
  </book>
  <book id="bk112">
    <author>Galos, Mike</author>
    <title>Visual Studio 7: A Comprehensive Guide</title>
    <genre>Computer</genre>
    <price>49.95</price>
    <publish_date>2001-04-16</publish_date>
    <description>Microsoft Visual Studio 7 is explored
    in depth, looking at how Visual Basic, Visual C++, C#,
    and ASP+ are integrated into a comprehensive development
    environment.</description>
  </book>
</catalog>
```

4. Create the `xml.go` file with the following content:

```go
package main

import (
  "encoding/xml"
  "fmt"
  "os"
)

type Book struct {
  Title string `xml:"title"`
  Author string `xml:"author"`
}

func main() {

  f, err := os.Open("data.xml")
  if err != nil {
    panic(err)
  }
  defer f.Close()
  decoder := xml.NewDecoder(f)

  // Read the book one by one
  books := make([]Book, 0)
  for {
    tok, _ := decoder.Token()
    if tok == nil {
      break
    }
    switch tp := tok.(type) {
      case xml.StartElement:
        if tp.Name.Local == "book" {
          // Decode the element to struct
          var b Book
          decoder.DecodeElement(&b, &tp)
          books = append(books, b)
        }
    }
  }
  fmt.Println(books)
}
```

5. Execute the code by `go run xml.go`.

6. See the output:

```
PROBLEMS    OUTPUT    DEBUG CONSOLE    TERMINAL    1: bash    +    🗑    ∧    ✕

Macbooks-MacBook-Pro:recipe12 radek$ go run xml.go
[{XML Developer's Guide Gambardella, Matthew} {Visual Studio 7: A Comprehensi
ve Guide Galos, Mike}]
Macbooks-MacBook-Pro:recipe12 radek$ ▌
```

How it works...

With the `NewDecoder` function of the `xml` package, the `Decoder` for the XML content is created.

By calling the `Token` method on the `Decoder`, the `xml.Token` is received. The `xml.Token` is the interface which holds the token type. The behavior of the code can be defined, based on the type. The sample code tests if the parsed `xml.StartElement` is one of the `book` elements. Then it partially parses the data into a `Book` structure. This way, the position of the pointer in the underlying `Reader` in the `Decoder` is shifted by the struct data, and the parsing can continue.

Extracting data from an incomplete JSON array

This recipe contains a very specific use case, where your program consumes the JSON from an unreliable source and the JSON contains an array of objects which has the beginning token [but the number of items in the array is very large, and the end of the JSON could be corrupted.

How to do it...

1. Open the console and create the folder `chapter05/recipe13`.

2. Navigate to the directory.

3. Create the `json.go` file with the following content:

```go
package main

import (
  "encoding/json"
  "fmt"
  "strings"
)

const js = `
  [
    {
      "name":"Axel",
      "lastname":"Fooley"
    },
    {
      "name":"Tim",
      "lastname":"Burton"
    },
    {
      "name":"Tim",
      "lastname":"Burton"
`

type User struct {
  Name string `json:"name"`
  LastName string `json:"lastname"`
}

func main() {

  userSlice := make([]User, 0)
  r := strings.NewReader(js)
  dec := json.NewDecoder(r)
  for {
    tok, err := dec.Token()
    if err != nil {
      break
    }
    if tok == nil {
      break
    }
    switch tp := tok.(type) {
      case json.Delim:
        str := tp.String()
        if str == "[" || str == "{" {
```

```
        for dec.More() {
          u := User{}
          err := dec.Decode(&u)
          if err == nil {
            userSlice = append(userSlice, u)
          } else {
            break
          }
        }
      }
    }
  }

  fmt.Println(userSlice)
}
```

4. Execute the code by `go run json.go`.
5. See the output:

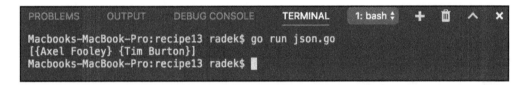

How it works...

Besides the `Unmarshall` function, the `json` package also contains the `Decoder` API. With `NewDecoder`, the `Decoder` could be created. By calling the `Token` method on the decoder, the underlying `Reader` is read and returns the `Token` interface. This could hold multiple values.

One of these is the `Delim` type, which is a rune containing one of the `{`, `[`, `]`, `}` characters. Based on this, the beginning of the JSON array is detected. With the `More` method on the decoder, more objects to decode could be detected.

6
Discovering the Filesystem

This chapter contains the following recipes:

- Getting file information
- Creating temporary files
- Writing the file
- Writing the file from multiple goroutines
- Listing a directory
- Changing file permissions
- Creating files and directories
- Filtering file listings
- Comparing two files
- Resolving the user home directory

Introduction

This chapter will lead you through the typical operations in files and directories. We will also touch on how to obtain the user home directory and create the temporary files for it.

 Check whether Go is properly installed. The *Getting ready* section from the *Retrieving Golang version* recipe of `Chapter 1`, *Interacting With Environment* will help you.

Getting file information

If you need to discover basic information about the accessed file, Go's standard library provides a way on how you can do this. This recipe shows how you can access this information.

How to do it...

1. Open the console and create the folder `chapter06/recipe01`.
2. Navigate to the directory.
3. Create the sample `test.file` with the content `This is test file`.
4. Create the `fileinfo.go` file with the following content:

```go
package main

import (
  "fmt"
  "os"
)

func main() {

  f, err := os.Open("test.file")
  if err != nil {
    panic(err)
  }
  fi, err := f.Stat()
  if err != nil {
    panic(err)
  }

  fmt.Printf("File name: %v\n", fi.Name())
  fmt.Printf("Is Directory: %t\n", fi.IsDir())
  fmt.Printf("Size: %d\n", fi.Size())
  fmt.Printf("Mode: %v\n", fi.Mode())

}
```

5. Execute the code by running `go run fileinfo.go` in the main Terminal.
6. You will see the following output:

```
PROBLEMS     TERMINAL      ...        1: bash        ‡  +  🗑  ∧  ☐  ✕
Macbooks-MacBook-Pro:recipe01 radek$ go run fileinfo.go
File name: test.file
Is Directory: false
Size: 18
Mode: -rw-r--r--
Macbooks-MacBook-Pro:recipe01 radek$
```

How it works...

The `os.File` type provides access to the `FileInfo` type via the `Stat` method. The `FileInfo` struct contains all the basic information about the file.

Creating temporary files

Temporary files are commonly used while running test cases or if your application needs to have a place to store short-term content such as user data uploads and currently processed data. This recipe will present the easiest way to create such a file or directory.

How to do it...

1. Open the console and create the folder `chapter06/recipe02`.
2. Navigate to the directory.
3. Create the `tempfile.go` file with the following content:

```go
package main

import "io/ioutil"
import "os"
import "fmt"

func main() {
    tFile, err := ioutil.TempFile("", "gostdcookbook")
    if err != nil {
```

```
        panic(err)
    }
    // The called is responsible for handling
    // the clean up.
    defer os.Remove(tFile.Name())

    fmt.Println(tFile.Name())

    // TempDir returns
    // the path in string.
    tDir, err := ioutil.TempDir("", "gostdcookbookdir")
    if err != nil {
        panic(err)
    }
    defer os.Remove(tDir)
    fmt.Println(tDir)


}
```

4. Execute the code by running `go run tempfile.go` in the main Terminal.

5. You will see the following output:

How it works...

The `ioutil` package contains the functions `TempFile` and `TempDir`. The `TempFile` function consumes the directory and the file prefix. The `os.File` with the underlying temporary file is returned. Note that the caller is responsible for cleaning out the file. The previous example uses the `os.Remove` function to do that.

The `TempDir` function works the same way. The difference is that the `string` with the path to the directory is returned.

The temp `file`/`dir` name is composed of the prefix and the random suffix. Multiple programs calling the `TempFile`/`Dir` function with the same arguments won't get the same result.

Writing the file

Writing a file is an essential task for every programmer; Go supports multiple ways on how you can do this. This recipe will show a few of them.

How to do it...

1. Open the console and create the folder `chapter06/recipe03`.
2. Navigate to the directory.
3. Create the `writefile.go` file with the following content:

```
package main

import (
  "io"
  "os"
  "strings"
)

func main() {

  f, err := os.Create("sample.file")
  if err != nil {
    panic(err)
  }
  defer f.Close()

  _, err = f.WriteString("Go is awesome!\n")
  if err != nil {
    panic(err)
  }

  _, err = io.Copy(f, strings.NewReader("Yeah! Go
                  is great.\n"))
  if err != nil {
    panic(err)
  }
}
```

4. Execute the code by running `go run writefile.go` in the main Terminal.

5. Check the content of the created `sample.file`:

```
PROBLEMS      TERMINAL      •••        1: bash      ⬍    +   🗑   ⌃   ⬜   ✕

Macbooks-MacBook-Pro:recipe03 radek$ cat sample.file
Go is awesome!
Yeah! Go is great.
Macbooks-MacBook-Pro:recipe03 radek$ ▮
```

How it works...

The `os.File` type implements the `Writer` interface, so writing to the file could be done by any option that uses the `Writer` interface. The preceding example uses the `WriteString` method of the `os.File` type. The `io.WriteString` method can also be used in general.

Writing the file from multiple goroutines

This recipe will show you how to safely write to the file from multiple goroutines.

How to do it...

1. Open the console and create the folder `chapter06/recipe04`.

2. Navigate to the directory.

3. Create the `syncwrite.go` file with the following content:

```go
package main

import (
  "fmt"
  "io"
  "os"
  "sync"
)

type SyncWriter struct {
  m sync.Mutex
```

```go
    Writer io.Writer
}

func (w *SyncWriter) Write(b []byte) (n int, err error) {
    w.m.Lock()
    defer w.m.Unlock()
    return w.Writer.Write(b)
}

var data = []string{
    "Hello!",
    "Ola!",
    "Ahoj!",
}

func main() {

    f, err := os.Create("sample.file")
    if err != nil {
        panic(err)
    }

    wr := &SyncWriter{sync.Mutex{}, f}
    wg := sync.WaitGroup{}
    for _, val := range data {
        wg.Add(1)
        go func(greetings string) {
            fmt.Fprintln(wr, greetings)
            wg.Done()
        }(val)
    }

    wg.Wait()
}
```

4. Execute the code by running `go run syncwrite.go` in the main Terminal.
5. Check the content of the created `sample.file`:

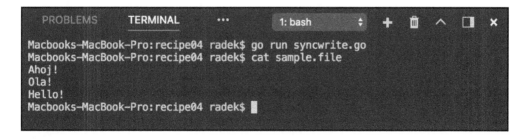

How it works...

Writing concurrently to a file is a problem that can end up with inconsistent file content. It is better to synchronize the writing to the file by using `Mutex` or any other synchronization primitive. This way, you ensure that only one goroutine at a time will be able to write to the file.

The preceding code creates a `Writer` with `Mutex`, which embeds the `Writer` (`os.File`, in this case), and for each `Write` call, internally locks the `Mutex` to provide exclusivity. After the write operation is complete, the `Mutex` primitive is unlocked naturally.

Listing a directory

This recipe will show you how to list directory content.

How to do it...

1. Open the console and create the folder `chapter06/recipe05`.
2. Navigate to the directory.
3. Create a directory named `folder`.
4. Create the `listdir.go` file with the following content:

```go
package main

import (
  "fmt"
  "io/ioutil"
  "os"
  "path/filepath"
)

func main() {

  fmt.Println("List by ReadDir")
  listDirByReadDir(".")
  fmt.Println()
  fmt.Println("List by Walk")
  listDirByWalk(".")
}
```

```go
func listDirByWalk(path string) {
    filepath.Walk(path, func(wPath string, info os.FileInfo,
                             err error) error {

        // Walk the given dir
        // without printing out.
        if wPath == path {
            return nil
        }

        // If given path is folder
        // stop list recursively and print as folder.
        if info.IsDir() {
            fmt.Printf("[%s]\n", wPath)
            return filepath.SkipDir
        }

        // Print file name
        if wPath != path {
            fmt.Println(wPath)
        }
        return nil
    })
}

func listDirByReadDir(path string) {
    lst, err := ioutil.ReadDir(path)
    if err != nil {
        panic(err)
    }
    for _, val := range lst {
        if val.IsDir() {
            fmt.Printf("[%s]\n", val.Name())
        } else {
            fmt.Println(val.Name())
        }
    }
}
```

5. Execute the code by running `go run listdir.go` in the main Terminal.
6. You will see the following output:

How it works...

The folder listing the example above uses two approaches. The first, simpler one is implemented by using the `listDirByReadDir` function and utilizes the `ReadDir` function from the `ioutil` package. This function returns the slice of `FileInfo` structs that represent the actual directory content. Note that the `ReadDir` function does not read the folders recursively. In fact, the `ReadDir` function internally uses the `Readdir` method of the `File` type in the `os` package.

On the other hand, the more complicated `listDirByWalk` uses the `filepath.Walk` function which consumes the path to be walked and has a function that processes each file or folder in any given path. The main difference is that the `Walk` function reads the directory recursively. The core part of this approach is the `WalkFunc` type, where its function is to consume the results of the listing. Note that the function blocks the recursive call on underlying folders by returning the `filepath.SkipDir` error. The `Walk` function also processes the called path at first, so you need to handle this as well (in this case, we skip the printing and return nil because we need to process this folder recursively).

Changing file permissions

This recipe illustrates how file permissions can be changed programmatically.

How to do it...

1. Open the console and create the folder `chapter06/recipe06`.
2. Navigate to the directory.
3. Create the `filechmod.go` file with the following content:

```go
package main

import (
  "fmt"
  "os"
)

func main() {

  f, err := os.Create("test.file")
  if err != nil {
    panic(err)
  }
  defer f.Close()

  // Obtain current permissions
  fi, err := f.Stat()
  if err != nil {
    panic(err)
  }
  fmt.Printf("File permissions %v\n", fi.Mode())

  // Change permissions
  err = f.Chmod(0777)
  if err != nil {
    panic(err)
  }
  fi, err = f.Stat()
  if err != nil {
    panic(err)
  }
  fmt.Printf("File permissions %v\n", fi.Mode())

}
```

4. Execute the code by running `go run filechmod.go` in the main Terminal.
5. You will see the following output:

```
PROBLEMS    TERMINAL    ...    1: bash    +  🗑  ^  🔲  ✕
Macbooks-MacBook-Pro:recipe06 radek$ go run filechmod.go
File permissions -rw-r--r--
File permissions -rwxrwxrwx
Macbooks-MacBook-Pro:recipe06 radek$ ▮
```

How it works...

The `Chmod` method of the `File` type in the `os` package can be used to change file permissions. The preceding example just creates the file and changes the permissions to `0777`.

Just note that the `fi.Mode()` is called twice because it extracts the permissions (`os.FileMode`) for the current state of the file.

The shortest way to change the permissions is by using the `os.Chmod` function, which does the same, but you do not need to obtain the `File` type in the code.

Creating files and directories

This recipe describes a few general ways you can create files and directories in code.

How to do it...

1. Open the console and create the folder `chapter06/recipe07`.
2. Navigate to the directory.
3. Create the `create.go` file with the following content:

```
package main

import (
  "os"
)
```

```go
func main() {

  f, err := os.Create("created.file")
  if err != nil {
    panic(err)
  }
  f.Close()

  f, err = os.OpenFile("created.byopen", os.O_CREATE|os.O_APPEND,
                       os.ModePerm)
  if err != nil {
    panic(err)
  }
  f.Close()

  err = os.Mkdir("createdDir", 0777)
  if err != nil {
    panic(err)
  }

  err = os.MkdirAll("sampleDir/path1/path2", 0777)
  if err != nil {
    panic(err)
  }

}
```

4. Execute the code by running `go run create.go` in the main Terminal.
5. List the content of the `chapter06/recipe07` directory:

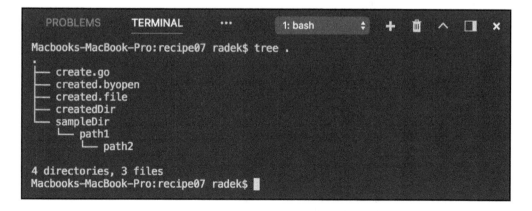

How it works...

The previous example represents four ways you can create a file or directory.
The os.Create function is the simplest way to create the file. By using this function, you will create the file with permissions such as 0666.

If you need to create the file with any other configuration of permissions, then the OpenFile function of the os package is the one to be used.

The directories can be created by using the Mkdir function of the os package. This way, a directory with given permissions is created. The second option is to use the MkdirAll function. This function also creates the directory, but if the given path contains non-exiting directories, then all directories in the path are created (it works the same as the -p option of Unix's mkdir utility).

Filtering file listings

This recipe shows you how to list the file paths, matching a given pattern. The list does not have to be from the same folder.

How to do it...

1. Open the console and create the folder chapter06/recipe08.
2. Navigate to the directory.
3. Create the filter.go file with the following content:

```
package main

import (
  "fmt"
  "os"
  "path/filepath"
)

func main() {

  for i := 1; i <= 6; i++ {
    _, err := os.Create(fmt.Sprintf("./test.file%d", i))
    if err != nil {
      fmt.Println(err)
```

```
      }
    }

    m, err := filepath.Glob("./test.file[1-3]")
    if err != nil {
      panic(err)
    }

    for _, val := range m {
      fmt.Println(val)
    }

    // Cleanup
    for i := 1; i <= 6; i++ {
      err := os.Remove(fmt.Sprintf("./test.file%d", i))
      if err != nil {
        fmt.Println(err)
      }
    }
  }
}
```

4. Execute the code by running go run filter.go in the main Terminal.

5. You will see the following output:

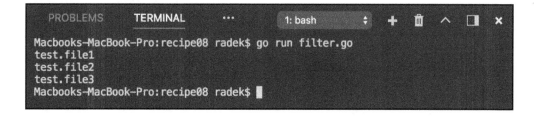

How it works...

To get the filtered file list which corresponds to the given pattern, the Glob function from the filepath package can be used. For the pattern syntax, see the documentation of the filepath.Match function (https://golang.org/pkg/path/filepath/#Match).

Note that the returning result of filepath.Glob is the slice of strings with matching paths.

See also

The *Listing a directory* recipe of this chapter, which shows a more generic approach where the `filepath.Walk` function can be used to list and filter the path too.

Comparing two files

This recipe gives you a hint on how to compare two files. The recipe will show you how to quickly determine whether the files are identical. The recipe will also present you with a way to find differences between the two.

How to do it...

1. Open the console and create the folder `chapter06/recipe09`.
2. Navigate to the directory.
3. Create the `comparison.go` file with the following content:

```go
package main

import (
  "bufio"
  "crypto/md5"
  "fmt"
  "io"
  "os"
)

var data = []struct {
  name string
  cont string
  perm os.FileMode
}{
  {"test1.file", "Hello\nGolang is great", 0666},
  {"test2.file", "Hello\nGolang is great", 0666},
  {"test3.file", "Not matching\nGolang is great\nLast line",
    0666},
}

func main() {

  files := []*os.File{}
```

```go
      for _, fData := range data {
        f, err := os.Create(fData.name)
        if err != nil {
          panic(err)
        }
        defer f.Close()
        _, err = io.WriteString(f, fData.cont)
        if err != nil {
          panic(err)
        }
        files = append(files, f)
      }

      // Compare by checksum
      checksums := []string{}
      for _, f := range files {
        f.Seek(0, 0) // reset to beginning of file
        sum, err := getMD5SumString(f)
        if err != nil {
          panic(err)
        }
        checksums = append(checksums, sum)
      }

      fmt.Println("### Comparing by checksum ###")
      compareCheckSum(checksums[0], checksums[1])
      compareCheckSum(checksums[0], checksums[2])

      fmt.Println("### Comparing line by line ###")
      files[0].Seek(0, 0)
      files[2].Seek(0, 0)
      compareFileByLine(files[0], files[2])

      // Cleanup
      for _, val := range data {
        os.Remove(val.name)
      }

    }

    func getMD5SumString(f *os.File) (string, error) {
      file1Sum := md5.New()
      _, err := io.Copy(file1Sum, f)
      if err != nil {
        return "", err
      }
      return fmt.Sprintf("%X", file1Sum.Sum(nil)), nil
    }
```

```go
func compareCheckSum(sum1, sum2 string) {
  match := "match"
  if sum1 != sum2 {
    match = " does not match"
  }
  fmt.Printf("Sum: %s and Sum: %s %s\n", sum1, sum2, match)
}

func compareLines(line1, line2 string) {
  sign := "o"
  if line1 != line2 {
    sign = "x"
  }
  fmt.Printf("%s | %s | %s \n", sign, line1, line2)
}

func compareFileByLine(f1, f2 *os.File) {
  sc1 := bufio.NewScanner(f1)
  sc2 := bufio.NewScanner(f2)

  for {
    sc1Bool := sc1.Scan()
    sc2Bool := sc2.Scan()
    if !sc1Bool && !sc2Bool {
      break
    }
    compareLines(sc1.Text(), sc2.Text())
  }
}
```

4. Execute the code by running `go run comparison.go` in the main Terminal.
5. You will see the following output:

```
PROBLEMS    TERMINAL    ···        1: bash    ⬍  +  🗑  ^  ▢  ✕

Macbooks-MacBook-Pro:recipe09 radek$ go run comparison.go
### Comparing by checksum ###
Sum: 5A07C1538087CD5B5C365DE52970E0A3 and Sum: 5A07C1538087CD5B5C365DE52970E0A3
match
Sum: 5A07C1538087CD5B5C365DE52970E0A3 and Sum: FED2EADA5D1D1EBF745DFDC7D1385E6C
 does not match
### Comparing line by line ###
x | Hello | Not matching
o | Golang is great | Golang is great
x |  | Last line
Macbooks-MacBook-Pro:recipe09 radek$ ▊
```

How it works...

The comparison of the two files can be done in a few ways. This recipe describes the two basic ones. The first one is by doing a comparison of the whole file by creating the checksum of the file.

The *Generating checksum* recipe of Chapter 3, *Dealing with Numbers* shows how you can create the checksum of the file. This way, the getMD5SumString function generates the checksum string, which is a hexadecimal representation of the byte result of MD5. The strings are then compared.

The second approach compares the files line by line (in this case, the string content). In case the lines are not matching, the x sign is included. This is the same way you can compare the binary content, but you will need to scan the file by blocks of bytes (byte slices).

Resolving the user home directory

It could be beneficial for the program to know the user's home directory, for example, in case you need to store a custom user configuration or any other data related to the user. This recipe will describe how you can find out the current user's home directory.

How to do it...

1. Open the console and create the folder chapter06/recipe10.
2. Navigate to the directory.
3. Create the home.go file with the following content:

```go
package main

import (
  "fmt"
  "log"
  "os/user"
)

func main() {
  usr, err := user.Current()
  if err != nil {
    log.Fatal(err)
  }
```

```
        fmt.Println("The user home directory: " + usr.HomeDir)
    }
```

4. Execute the code by running `go run home.go` in the main Terminal.
5. You will see the following output:

How it works...

The `os/user` package contains the `Current` function, which provides the `os.User` type pointer. The `User` contains the `HomeDir` property, which contains the path of the current user's home directory.

> Note that this won't work for the cross-compiled code because the implementation depends on the native code.

7
Connecting the Network

This chapter contains the following recipes:

- Resolving local IP addresses
- Connecting to the remote server
- Resolving the domain by IP address and vice versa
- Connecting to the HTTP server
- Parsing and building a URL
- Creating an HTTP request
- Reading and writing HTTP headers
- Handling HTTP redirects
- Consuming the RESTful API
- Sending a simple email
- Calling the JSON-RPC service

Introduction

This chapter is all about networking. Most of the recipes in this chapter are focused on the client side. We will go through how to resolve basic information about the network on the machine, domain names and IP resolution, and connecting through TCP-related protocols such as HTTP and SMTP. Finally, we will make a remote procedure call via JSON-RCP 1.0 with the use of the standard library.

Check whether Go is properly installed. The *Getting ready* section from the *Retrieving Golang version* recipe from `Chapter 1`, *Interacting With Environment,* will help you. Verify if any other application blocks the `7070` port.

Resolving local IP addresses

This recipe explains how to retrieve IP addresses from available local interfaces.

How to do it...

1. Open the console and create the folder `chapter07/recipe01`.
2. Navigate to the directory.
3. Create the `interfaces.go` file with the following content:

```
package main

import (
  "fmt"
  "net"
)

func main() {

  // Get all network interfaces
  interfaces, err := net.Interfaces()
  if err != nil {
    panic(err)
  }

  for _, interf := range interfaces {
    // Resolve addresses
    // for each interface
    addrs, err := interf.Addrs()
    if err != nil {
      panic(err)
    }
    fmt.Println(interf.Name)
    for _, add := range addrs {
      if ip, ok := add.(*net.IPNet); ok {
```

```
        fmt.Printf("\t%v\n", ip)
      }
    }


    }
  }
```

4. Execute the code by running `go run interfaces.go` in the main Terminal.
5. You will see the following output:

How it works...

The net package contains the `Interfaces` function, which lists the network interfaces as a slice of the `Interface` struct. The `Interface` struct has the `Addrs` method, which lists the available network addresses. This way, you can list the addresses by their interfaces.

Another option is to use the `InterfaceAddrs` function of the `net` package, which provides the slice of structs that implement the `Addr` interface. This provides you with methods to obtain the information you want.

Connecting to the remote server

TCP-based protocols are the most significant protocols used in network communication. Just as a reminder, HTTP, FTP, SMTP, and other protocols are part of this group. This recipe gives you an insight on how to connect to the TCP server in general.

How to do it...

1. Open the console and create the folder `chapter07/recipe02`.
2. Navigate to the directory.
3. Create the `tcpclient.go` file with the following content:

```go
package main

import (
  "bufio"
  "context"
  "fmt"
  "io"
  "net"
  "net/http"
  "time"
)

type StringServer string

func (s StringServer) ServeHTTP(rw http.ResponseWriter,
                                req *http.Request) {
  rw.Write([]byte(string(s)))
}

func createServer(addr string) http.Server {
  return http.Server{
    Addr: addr,
    Handler: StringServer("HELLO GOPHER!\n"),
  }
}

const addr = "localhost:7070"

func main() {
  s := createServer(addr)
  go s.ListenAndServe()
```

```go
// Connect with plain TCP
conn, err := net.Dial("tcp", addr)
if err != nil {
  panic(err)
}
defer conn.Close()

_, err = io.WriteString(conn, "GET / HTTP/1.1\r\nHost:
                        localhost:7070\r\n\r\n")
if err != nil {
  panic(err)
}

scanner := bufio.NewScanner(conn)
conn.SetReadDeadline(time.Now().Add(time.Second))
for scanner.Scan() {
  fmt.Println(scanner.Text())
}

ctx, _ := context.WithTimeout(context.Background(),
                              5*time.Second)
s.Shutdown(ctx)

}
```

4. Execute the code by running `go run tcpclient.go` in the main Terminal.
5. You will see the following output:

How it works...

The net package contains the `Dial` function, which consumes the network type and address. In the previous example, the network is `tcp` and the address is `localhost:8080`.

Once the `Dial` function is successful, the `Conn` type is returned, which serves as a reference to the opened socket. The `Conn` interface also defines the `Read` and `Write` functions, so they can be used as `Writer` and `Reader` functions for writing and reading from the socket. Finally, the sample code uses `Scanner` to obtain the response. Note that the `Scanner`, in this case, works because of the brake lines. Otherwise, the more generic `Read` method should be used. In the example, the `Read` deadline is set via the `SetReadDeadline` method. The important thing about this is that the deadline is not a duration, but a `Time`. This means the deadline is set as a time point in the future. If you are reading the data from a socket in a loop and need to set the read timeout to 10 seconds, each iteration should contain code such as `conn.SetReadDeadline(time.Now().Add(10*time.Second))`.

Just to enlighten the whole code sample, the HTTP server from the `HTTP` standard package is used as a counterpart to the client. This part is covered in a separate recipe.

Resolving the domain by IP address and vice versa

This recipe will introduce you to how you can translate IP addresses into host addresses and vice versa.

How to do it...

1. Open the console and create the folder `chapter07/recipe03`.
2. Navigate to the directory.
3. Create the `lookup.go` file with the following content:

```
package main

import (
  "fmt"
  "net"
)

func main() {

  // Resolve by IP
  addrs, err := net.LookupAddr("127.0.0.1")
  if err != nil {
```

```
      panic(err)
    }

    for _, addr := range addrs {
      fmt.Println(addr)
    }

    //Resolve by address
    ips, err := net.LookupIP("localhost")
    if err != nil {
      panic(err)
    }

    for _, ip := range ips {
      fmt.Println(ip.String())
    }
}
```

4. Execute the code by running `go run lookup.go` in the main Terminal.
5. You will see the following output:

How it works...

The resolution of the domain name from the IP address can be done with the `LookupAddr` function from the `net` package. To find out the `IP` address from the domain name, the `LookupIP` function is applied.

Connecting to the HTTP server

The previous recipe, *Connecting to the remote server*, gave us an insight into how to connect the TCP server at a lower level. In this recipe, communication with the HTTP server at a higher level will be shown.

How to do it...

1. Open the console and create the folder `chapter07/recipe04`.
2. Navigate to the directory.
3. Create the `http.go` file with the following content:

```go
package main

import (
  "fmt"
  "io/ioutil"
  "net/http"
  "net/url"
  "strings"
)

type StringServer string

func (s StringServer) ServeHTTP(rw http.ResponseWriter,
                                req *http.Request) {
  req.ParseForm()
  fmt.Printf("Received form data: %v\n", req.Form)
  rw.Write([]byte(string(s)))
}

func createServer(addr string) http.Server {
  return http.Server{
    Addr: addr,
    Handler: StringServer("Hello world"),
  }
}

const addr = "localhost:7070"

func main() {
  s := createServer(addr)
  go s.ListenAndServe()

  useRequest()
  simplePost()

}

func simplePost() {
  res, err := http.Post("http://localhost:7070",
                "application/x-www-form-urlencoded",
```

```
                        strings.NewReader("name=Radek&surname=Sohlich"))
  if err != nil {
    panic(err)
  }

  data, err := ioutil.ReadAll(res.Body)
  if err != nil {
    panic(err)
  }
  res.Body.Close()
  fmt.Println("Response from server:" + string(data))
}

func useRequest() {

  hc := http.Client{}
  form := url.Values{}
  form.Add("name", "Radek")
  form.Add("surname", "Sohlich")

  req, err := http.NewRequest("POST",
               "http://localhost:7070",
               strings.NewReader(form.Encode()))
               req.Header.Add("Content-Type",
               "application/x-www-form-urlencoded")

  res, err := hc.Do(req)

  if err != nil {
    panic(err)
  }

  data, err := ioutil.ReadAll(res.Body)
  if err != nil {
    panic(err)
  }
  res.Body.Close()
  fmt.Println("Response from server:" + string(data))
}
```

4. Execute the code by running `go run http.go` in the main Terminal.
5. You will see the following output:

```
PROBLEMS     TERMINAL      ...              1: bash
Macbooks-MacBook-Pro:recipe04 radek$ go run http.go
Received form data: map[surname:[Sohlich] name:[Radek]]
Response from server:Hello world
Received form data: map[name:[Radek] surname:[Sohlich]]
Response from server:Hello world
Macbooks-MacBook-Pro:recipe04 radek$
```

How it works...

Connecting to the HTTP server can be done with help of the `net/http` package. Naturally, there are more ways you can achieve this, but the code above illustrates two of the most common approaches. The first option implemented the `simplePost` function, and illustrates the use of a default client. The POST method is chosen here as it is more complex than GET. The `Post` method accepts the URL, content type, and body in the form of `Reader`. Invoking the `Post` function immediately requests the server and returns the result.

 Note that the `Post` method is just wrapping a function that uses the `http.DefaultClient` in its implementation. The `net/http` package also contains the `Get` function.

The `useRequest` function implements the same functionality, but with the use of a more customizable API and its own instance of `Client`. The implementation utilizes the `NewRequest` function to create the request based on these given arguments: method, URL, and request body. The content type must be set separately to the `Header` property. The request is executed with the `Do` method, which is created on the `Client`.

See also

The *Creating an HTTP request* recipe that will help you assemble a request in detail.

Parsing and building a URL

In many cases, it is better to manipulate a URL with the use of handy tools than trying to handle it as a simple string. Go standard libraries naturally contain the utilities to manipulate a URL. This recipe will go through some of these major functions.

How to do it...

1. Open the console and create the folder `chapter07/recipe05`.
2. Navigate to the directory.
3. Create the `url.go` file with the following content:

```go
package main

import (
  "encoding/json"
  "fmt"
  "net/url"
)

func main() {

  u := &url.URL{}
  u.Scheme = "http"
  u.Host = "localhost"
  u.Path = "index.html"
  u.RawQuery = "id=1&name=John"
  u.User = url.UserPassword("admin", "1234")

  fmt.Printf("Assembled URL:\n%v\n\n\n", u)

  parsedURL, err := url.Parse(u.String())
  if err != nil {
    panic(err)
  }
  jsonURL, err := json.Marshal(parsedURL)
  if err != nil {
    panic(err)
  }
  fmt.Println("Parsed URL:")
  fmt.Println(string(jsonURL))

}
```

4. Execute the code by running `go run url.go` in the main Terminal.
5. You will see the following output:

```
PROBLEMS    TERMINAL    ...          1: bash    +  ⌃  ◻  ✕

Macbooks-MacBook-Pro:recipe05 radek$ go run url.go
Assembled URL:
http://admin:1234@localhost/index.html?id=1&name=John


Parsed URL:
{"Scheme":"http","Opaque":"","User":{},"Host":"localhost","Path":"/index.html",
"RawPath":"","ForceQuery":false,"RawQuery":"id=1\u0026name=John","Fragment":""}
Macbooks-MacBook-Pro:recipe05 radek$ █
```

How it works...

The `net/url` package is designed to help you with the manipulation and parsing of a URL. The `URL` struct contains the necessary fields to put a URL together. With the `String` method of the `URL` struct, the transformation to a simple string can be easily done.

When the string representation is available and additional manipulation is needed, the `Parse` function of `net/url` can be utilized. This way, the string can be transformed to a `URL` struct, and the underlying URL can be modified.

Creating an HTTP request

This recipe will show you how to construct a HTTP request with specific parameters.

How to do it...

1. Open the console and create the folder `chapter07/recipe06`.
2. Navigate to the directory.

3. Create the `request.go` file with the following content:

```go
package main

import (
  "fmt"
  "io/ioutil"
  "net/http"
  "net/url"
  "strings"
)

type StringServer string

func (s StringServer) ServeHTTP(rw http.ResponseWriter,
                                req *http.Request) {
  req.ParseForm()
  fmt.Printf("Received form data: %v\n", req.Form)
  fmt.Printf("Received header: %v\n", req.Header)
  rw.Write([]byte(string(s)))
}

func createServer(addr string) http.Server {
  return http.Server{
    Addr: addr,
    Handler: StringServer("Hello world"),
  }
}

const addr = "localhost:7070"

func main() {
  s := createServer(addr)
  go s.ListenAndServe()

  form := url.Values{}
  form.Set("id", "5")
  form.Set("name", "Wolfgang")

  req, err := http.NewRequest(http.MethodPost,
                    "http://localhost:7070",
                    strings.NewReader(form.Encode()))

  if err != nil {
    panic(err)
  }
  req.Header.Set("Content-Type",
```

```
                    "application/x-www-form-urlencoded")

    res, err := http.DefaultClient.Do(req)
    if err != nil {
      panic(err)
    }
    data, err := ioutil.ReadAll(res.Body)
    if err != nil {
      panic(err)
    }
    res.Body.Close()
    fmt.Println("Response from server:" + string(data))

  }
```

4. Execute the code by running go run request.go in the main Terminal.
5. You will see the following output:

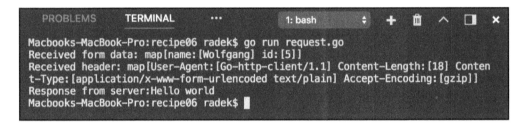

How it works...

The more complex way to construct the request is presented in the sample code. With the NewRequest method of the net/http package, the pointer to the Request struct is returned. The function consumes the method's request, URL, and body of the request. Notice the way the form is built. Instead of using the plain string, the url.Values struct is used. Finally, the Encode method is called to encode the given form values. The headers are set via the http.Header property of the request.

Reading and writing HTTP headers

The previous recipe describes how you can create a HTTP request in general. This recipe will go into detail on how to read and write request headers.

How to do it...

1. Open the console and create the folder chapter07/recipe07.
2. Navigate to the directory.
3. Create the headers.go file with the following content:

```
package main

import (
  "fmt"
  "net/http"
)

func main() {

  header := http.Header{}

  // Using the header as slice
  header.Set("Auth-X", "abcdef1234")
  header.Add("Auth-X", "defghijkl")
  fmt.Println(header)

  // retrieving slice of values in header
  resSlice := header["Auth-X"]
  fmt.Println(resSlice)

  // get the first value
  resFirst := header.Get("Auth-X")
  fmt.Println(resFirst)

  // replace all existing values with
  // this one
  header.Set("Auth-X", "newvalue")
  fmt.Println(header)

  // Remove header
  header.Del("Auth-X")
  fmt.Println(header)

}
```

4. Execute the code by running `go run headers.go` in the main Terminal.
5. You will see the following output:

```
PROBLEMS    TERMINAL    ...              1: bash       +  🗑  ^  ☐  ✕

Macbooks-MacBook-Pro:recipe07 radek$ go run headers.go
map[Auth-X:[abcdef1234 defghijkl]]
[abcdef1234 defghijkl]
abcdef1234
map[Auth-X:[newvalue]]
map[]
Macbooks-MacBook-Pro:recipe07 radek$ ▮
```

How it works...

The headers in the `http` package are, in fact, represented as `map[string][]string`, and this way, the `Header` type must be handled. The preceding code shows how to set and read the header values. The important thing about the header is that the value of the header key is the `string` slice. So, each key in a header can contain multiple values.

The `Set` method of the `Header` type sets the one-item slice under the given key. On the other hand, the `Add` method appends the values to the slice.

Using the `Get` method will retrieve the first value from the slice under the given key. If the whole slice is needed, the `Header` needs to be handled as a map. The whole header key can be removed by using the `Del` method.

 Both the server and client use the `Request` and `Header` type of `http` package so that handling is the same on the server side and on the client side.

Handling HTTP redirects

In some cases, you need more control over how redirects are handled. This recipe will show you the mechanism which the Go client implements so that you have more control over handling HTTP redirects.

How to do it...

1. Open the console and create the folder `chapter07/recipe08`.
2. Navigate to the directory.
3. Create the `redirects.go` file with the following content:

```go
package main

import (
  "fmt"
  "net/http"
)

const addr = "localhost:7070"

type RedirecServer struct {
  redirectCount int
}

func (s *RedirecServer) ServeHTTP(rw http.ResponseWriter,
                                  req *http.Request) {
  s.redirectCount++
  fmt.Println("Received header: " +
              req.Header.Get("Known-redirects"))
  http.Redirect(rw, req, fmt.Sprintf("/redirect%d",
                s.redirectCount), http.StatusTemporaryRedirect)
}

func main() {
  s := http.Server{
    Addr: addr,
    Handler: &RedirecServer{0},
  }
  go s.ListenAndServe()

  client := http.Client{}
  redirectCount := 0

  // If the count of redirects is reached
  // than return error.
  client.CheckRedirect = func(req *http.Request,
                          via []*http.Request) error {
    fmt.Println("Redirected")
    if redirectCount > 2 {
      return fmt.Errorf("Too many redirects")
    }
```

```
        req.Header.Set("Known-redirects", fmt.Sprintf("%d",
                           redirectCount))
        redirectCount++
        for _, prReq := range via {
          fmt.Printf("Previous request: %v\n", prReq.URL)
        }
        return nil
      }

    _, err := client.Get("http://" + addr)
    if err != nil {
      panic(err)
    }
  }
```

4. Execute the code by running `go run redirects.go` in the main Terminal.
5. You will see the following output:

How it works...

The `Client` of the `http` package contains the `CheckRedirect` field. The field is a function that has the `req` and `via` parameters. `req` is the upcoming request and `via` refers to the previous requests. This way, you can modify the request after the redirect. In the previous example, the `Known-redirects` header is modified.

In case the `CheckRedirect` function returns the error, the last response with a closed body accompanied with a wrapped error is returned. In case the `http.ErrUseLastResponse` is returned, the last response is returned, but the body is not closed so it is possible to read it.

> By default, the `CheckRedirect` property is nil. In this case, it has a limit of 10 redirects. After this count, redirecting is stopped.

Consuming the RESTful API

The RESTful API is the most common way applications and servers provide access to their services. This recipe will show you how it can be consumed with the help of a HTTP client from the standard library.

How to do it...

1. Open the console and create the folder `chapter07/recipe09`.
2. Navigate to the directory.
3. Create the `rest.go` file with the following content:

```go
package main

import (
  "encoding/json"
  "fmt"
  "io"
  "io/ioutil"
  "net/http"
  "strconv"
  "strings"
)
```

```go
const addr = "localhost:7070"

type City struct {
  ID string
  Name string `json:"name"`
  Location string `json:"location"`
}

func (c City) toJson() string {
  return fmt.Sprintf(`{"name":"%s","location":"%s"}`,
                        c.Name, c.Location)
}

func main() {
  s := createServer(addr)
  go s.ListenAndServe()

  cities, err := getCities()
  if err != nil {
    panic(err)
  }
  fmt.Printf("Retrived cities: %v\n", cities)

  city, err := saveCity(City{"", "Paris", "France"})
  if err != nil {
    panic(err)
  }
  fmt.Printf("Saved city: %v\n", city)

}

func saveCity(city City) (City, error) {
  r, err := http.Post("http://"+addr+"/cities",
                        "application/json",
                          strings.NewReader(city.toJson()))
  if err != nil {
    return City{}, err
  }
  defer r.Body.Close()
  return decodeCity(r.Body)
}

func getCities() ([]City, error) {
  r, err := http.Get("http://" + addr + "/cities")
  if err != nil {
    return nil, err
  }
  defer r.Body.Close()
```

```
      return decodeCities(r.Body)
  }

  func decodeCity(r io.Reader) (City, error) {
    city := City{}
    dec := json.NewDecoder(r)
    err := dec.Decode(&city)
    return city, err
  }

func decodeCities(r io.Reader) ([]City, error) {
  cities := []City{}
  dec := json.NewDecoder(r)
  err := dec.Decode(&cities)
  return cities, err
}

func createServer(addr string) http.Server {
  cities := []City{City{"1", "Prague", "Czechia"},
                   City{"2", "Bratislava", "Slovakia"}}
  mux := http.NewServeMux()
  mux.HandleFunc("/cities", func(w http.ResponseWriter,
                                 r *http.Request) {
    enc := json.NewEncoder(w)
    if r.Method == http.MethodGet {
      enc.Encode(cities)
    } else if r.Method == http.MethodPost {
      data, err := ioutil.ReadAll(r.Body)
      if err != nil {
        http.Error(w, err.Error(), 500)
      }
      r.Body.Close()
      city := City{}
      json.Unmarshal(data, &city)
      city.ID = strconv.Itoa(len(cities) + 1)
      cities = append(cities, city)
      enc.Encode(city)
    }

  })
  return http.Server{
    Addr: addr,
    Handler: mux,
  }
}
```

4. Execute the code by running `go run rest.go` in the main Terminal.
5. You will see the following output:

```
PROBLEMS     TERMINAL     ...          1: bash        +  🗑  ∧  ☐  ✕

Macbooks-MacBook-Pro:recipe09 radek$ go run rest.go
Retrived cities: [{1 Prague Czechia} {2 Bratislava Slovakia}]
Saved city: {3 Paris France}
Macbooks-MacBook-Pro:recipe09 radek$ ▊
```

How it works...

The preceding sample code shows what the REST API could look like and how it could be consumed. Note that the `decodeCity` and `decodeCities` functions benefit from the fact that the `Body` of the request implements the `Reader` interface. The deserialization of the structures is done via `json.Decoder`.

Sending a simple email

This recipe will give you a brief description on how to use the standard library to connect to the SMTP server and send an email.

Getting ready

In this recipe, we will use a Google Gmail account to send the email message. With a few configurations, this recipe will be useful for other SMTP servers as well.

How to do it...

1. Open the console and create the folder `chapter07/recipe10`.
2. Navigate to the directory.
3. Create the `smtp.go` file with the following content:

```
package main

import (
```

```go
    "crypto/tls"
    "fmt"
    "net/smtp"
)

func main() {

  var email string
  fmt.Println("Enter username for smtp: ")
  fmt.Scanln(&email)

  var pass string
  fmt.Println("Enter password for smtp: ")
  fmt.Scanln(&pass)

  auth := smtp.PlainAuth("", email, pass, "smtp.gmail.com")

  c, err := smtp.Dial("smtp.gmail.com:587")
  if err != nil {
    panic(err)
  }
  defer c.Close()
  config := &tls.Config{ServerName: "smtp.gmail.com"}

  if err = c.StartTLS(config); err != nil {
    panic(err)
  }

  if err = c.Auth(auth); err != nil {
    panic(err)
  }

  if err = c.Mail(email); err != nil {
    panic(err)
  }
  if err = c.Rcpt(email); err != nil {
    panic(err)
  }

  w, err := c.Data()
  if err != nil {
    panic(err)
  }

  msg := []byte("Hello this is content")
  if _, err := w.Write(msg); err != nil {
    panic(err)
  }
```

```
       err = w.Close()
       if err != nil {
         panic(err)
       }
       err = c.Quit()

       if err != nil {
         panic(err)
       }

    }
```

4. Execute the code by running `go run smtp.go` in the main Terminal.
5. Enter the account's email (Google account) and hit *Enter*.
6. Enter the password for the account and hit *Enter*.
7. You will see the following output before checking your email box:

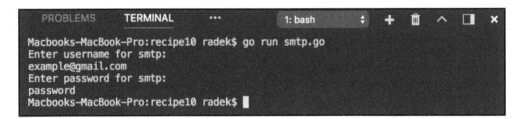

How it works...

The `smtp` package provides the basic functionality to interact with the SMTP server. The `Dial` function provides the client. The most significant methods of the client are `Mail`, which sets the sender mail, `Rcpt`, which sets the recipients mail, and `Data`, which provides the `Writer`, where the content of the mail can be written. Finally, the `Quit` method sends QUIT and closes the connection to the server.

The previous example uses a secured connection to the SMTP server so the `Auth` method of the client is utilized to set the authentication, and the `StartTLS` method is called to start a secured connection to the server.

Note that the `Auth` structure is created separately with the `PlainAuth` function of the `smtp` package.

Calling the JSON-RPC service

This recipe will illustrate how procedures via the JSON-RPC protocol can be called with use of the standard library.

How to do it...

1. Open the console and create the folder `chapter07/recipe11`.
2. Navigate to the directory.
3. Create the `jsonrpc.go` file with the following content:

```
package main

import (
  "log"
  "net"
  "net/rpc"
  "net/rpc/jsonrpc"
)

type Args struct {
  A, B int
}

type Result int

type RpcServer struct{}

func (t RpcServer) Add(args *Args, result *Result) error {
  log.Printf("Adding %d to %d\n", args.A, args.B)
  *result = Result(args.A + args.B)
  return nil
}

const addr = ":7070"

func main() {
  go createServer(addr)
  client, err := jsonrpc.Dial("tcp", addr)
  if err != nil {
    panic(err)
  }
  defer client.Close()
```

```
        args := &Args{
          A: 2,
          B: 3,
        }
        var result Result
        err = client.Call("RpcServer.Add", args, &result)
        if err != nil {
          log.Fatalf("error in RpcServer", err)
        }
        log.Printf("%d+%d=%d\n", args.A, args.B, result)
      }

      func createServer(addr string) {
        server := rpc.NewServer()
        err := server.Register(RpcServer{})
        if err != nil {
          panic(err)
        }
        l, e := net.Listen("tcp", addr)
        if e != nil {
          log.Fatalf("Couldn't start listening on %s errors: %s",
                    addr, e)
        }
        for {
          conn, err := l.Accept()
          if err != nil {
            log.Fatal(err)
          }
          go server.ServeCodec(jsonrpc.NewServerCodec(conn))
        }
      }
```

4. Execute the code by running `go run jsonrpc.go` in the main Terminal.
5. You will see the following output:

How it works...

Go's standard library implements JSON-RPC 1.0 as part of its built-in packages. The `jsonrpc` package implements the function `Dial`, which produces the client for calling remote procedures. The client itself contains the `Call` method, which accepts the procedure call, arguments, and the pointer where the result is stored.

The `createServer` will create a sample server to test the client call.

> The HTTP protocol can be used as a transport layer for JSON-RPC. The `net/rpc` package contains the `DialHTTP` function, which is able to create the client and call the remote procedures.

8
Working with Databases

This chapter contains the following recipes:

- Connecting the database
- Validating the connection
- Executing statements
- Operating with prepared statements
- Canceling the pending query
- Reading query result metadata
- Retrieving data from query result
- Parsing query result into map
- Handling transactions
- Executing stored procedures and functions

Introduction

Each database server has its own specifics and also, the protocols are different. Naturally, the communication with the database within the language library must be customized to work with the specific protocol.

The Go standard library provides a unified API for communication and operations on the database server. This API is located in the `sql` package. To use the specific database server, the driver must be imported. This driver needs to be `sql` package-compliant. This way, you will be able to benefit from the unified approach. In this chapter, we will describe the basics of database operations, transaction handling, and finally, how to use the stored procedures. Note that we are going to illustrate the approach on the PostgreSQL database, but the approaches are applicable to most other databases.

Connecting the database

The essential part of working with the database is the connection to the database itself. The Go standard package covers only the abstraction on how the interaction with the database works, and a third-party driver must be used.

In this recipe, we will show how to connect to the PostgreSQL database. However, the approach is applicable to all other databases whose driver implements the standard API.

Getting ready

Verify if Go is properly installed by calling the `go version` command in your Terminal. If the command fails, do the following:

- Pull the PostgreSQL driver by `go get -u github.com/lib/pq`
- Install the PostgreSQL database server (optionally use a Docker image instead of installing to your host system)
- We will use default user `postgres` with password `postgres`
- Create a database named `example`

How to do it...

1. Open the console and create the folder `chapter08/recipe01`.
2. Navigate to the directory.
3. Create the `connect.go` file with the following content:

```go
package main

import (
  "database/sql"
  "fmt"

  _ "github.com/lib/pq"
)

func main() {
  connStr := "postgres://postgres:postgres@
              localhost:5432/example?sslmode=disable"
  db, err := sql.Open("postgres", connStr)
  if err != nil {
```

```
        panic(err)
    }
    defer db.Close()
    err = db.Ping()
    if err != nil {
        panic(err)
    }
    fmt.Println("Ping OK")
}
```

4. Execute the code by `go run connect.go`.

5. See the output:

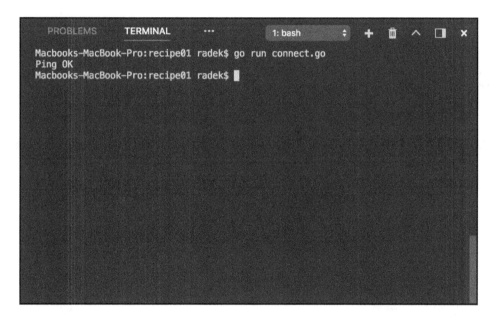

How it works...

The standard lib package, `database/sql`, provides the `Open` function to initialize the connection to the database with the driver name and connection details (connection URL in this case). Note that the `Open` function does not create the connection immediately, and may only validate the parameters passed to the function.

The connection to the database could be verified by the `Ping` method, which is available in the returned `DB` struct pointer.

The driver itself is initialized in the init function of the driver package. The driver registers itself with the driver name by the Register function of the sql package. The github.com/lib/pq driver registers itself as postgres.

Validating the connection

The connections to the database in the driver implementation may be pooled, and it is possible that the connection pulled out of the pool is broken. This recipe will show how to verify if the connection is alive.

Getting ready

Verify if Go is properly installed by calling the go version command in your Terminal. If the command fails, follow the *Getting ready* section in the first recipe of this chapter.

How to do it...

1. Open the console and create the folder chapter08/recipe02.
2. Navigate to the directory.
3. Create the verify.go file with the following content:

```go
package main

import (
  "context"
  "database/sql"
  "fmt"
  "time"

  _ "github.com/lib/pq"
)

func main() {
  connStr := "postgres://postgres:postgres@
              localhost:5432/example?sslmode=disable"
  db, err := sql.Open("postgres", connStr)
  if err != nil {
    panic(err)
  }
```

```
defer db.Close()
err = db.Ping()
if err != nil {
  panic(err)
}
fmt.Println("Ping OK.")
ctx, _ := context.WithTimeout(context.Background(),
                              time.Nanosecond)
err = db.PingContext(ctx)
if err != nil {
  fmt.Println("Error: " + err.Error())
}

// Verify the connection is
conn, err := db.Conn(context.Background())
if err != nil {
  panic(err)
}
defer conn.Close()
err = conn.PingContext(context.Background())
if err != nil {
  panic(err)
}
fmt.Println("Connection Ping OK.")

}
```

4. Execute the code by `go run verify.go`.

5. See the output:

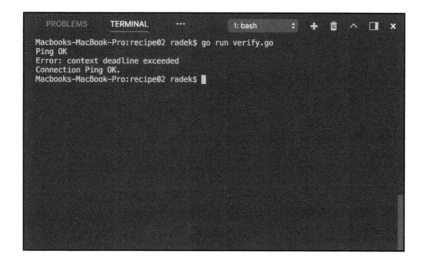

How it works...

As mentioned in the previous recipe, *Connecting the database*, the Open function may just verify the connection details, but it is not mandatory to connect the database immediately. The actual connection to the database is usually lazy loaded and it is created by the first execution of statement against the database.

The pointer to the DB structure provides the Ping method, which usually does an idempotent call to the database. The variation to the Ping method is PingContext, which just adds the ability to cancel or time out the database call. Note that if the Ping function fails, the connection is removed from the database pool.

The pointer to the DB struct also provides the method Conn to retrieve the connection from the database pool. By using the connection, you are actually guaranteed that the same database session is used. In the same way the pointer to the DB struct contains the PingContext method, the Conn pointer provides the PingContext method to check if the connection is still alive.

Executing statements

In previous recipes, we have gone through how to connect and validate the connection to the database. This recipe will describe how to execute statements against the database.

Getting ready

Verify if Go is properly installed by calling the go version command in your Terminal. If the command fails, follow the *Getting ready* section in the first recipe of this chapter.

Set up the PostgreSQL server, as mentioned in the first recipe of this chapter.

How to do it...

1. Run the following SQL script against your sample database:

```
DROP TABLE IF EXISTS post;
CREATE TABLE post (
  ID serial,
  TITLE varchar(40),
```

```
    CONTENT varchar(255),
    CONSTRAINT pk_post PRIMARY KEY(ID)
);
SELECT * FROM post;
```

2. Open the console and create the folder `chapter08/recipe03`.
3. Navigate to the directory.
4. Create the `statement.go` file with the following content:

```
package main

import (
  "database/sql"
  "fmt"
  _ "github.com/lib/pq"
)

const sel = "SELECT * FROM post;"
const trunc = "TRUNCATE TABLE post;"
const ins = "INSERT INTO post(ID,TITLE,CONTENT)
              VALUES (1,'Title 1','Content 1'),
              (2,'Title 2','Content 2') "

func main() {
  db := createConnection()
  defer db.Close()

  _, err := db.Exec(trunc)
  if err != nil {
    panic(err)
  }
  fmt.Println("Table truncated.")
  r, err := db.Exec(ins)
  if err != nil {
    panic(err)
  }
  affected, err := r.RowsAffected()
  if err != nil {
    panic(err)
  }
  fmt.Printf("Inserted rows count: %d\n",
              affected)

  rs, err := db.Query(sel)
  if err != nil {
    panic(err)
  }
```

```
count := 0
for rs.Next() {
  count++
}
fmt.Printf("Total of %d was selected.\n", count)
}

func createConnection() *sql.DB {
  connStr := "postgres://postgres:postgres@
            localhost:5432/example?sslmode=disable"
  db, err := sql.Open("postgres", connStr)
  if err != nil {
    panic(err)
  }
  err = db.Ping()
  if err != nil {
    panic(err)
  }
  return db
}
```

5. Execute the code by `go run statement.go`.

6. See the output:

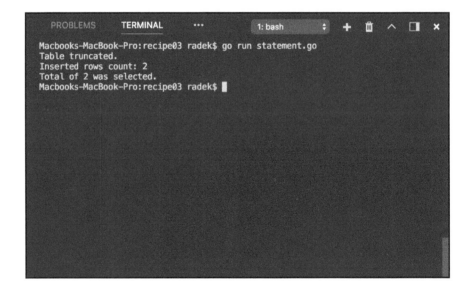

How it works...

Generally, there are two types of statements that we can execute against the database. With the first type of statements we do not expect any rows as a result and finally, we get no output or just a number of affected rows. This type of statement is executed by the `Exec` method on the `DB` struct pointer. In the preceding sample code, we have the `TRUNCATE` and `INSERT` statements. But this way, the DDL and DCL statements could be executed too.

There are four main categories of statements:

- **DDL (Data Definition Language)**: This language allows you to create and modify the database scheme
- **DML (Data Modeling Language)**: This language helps you to modify the data
- **DCL (Data Control Language)**: This language defines the access control over the objects
- **TCL (Transaction Control Language)**: This language controls the transaction.

The second type is the statement where we are expecting the result in the form of rows; these are usually called queries. This type of statement is usually executed by the `Query` or `QueryContext` method.

Operations with prepared statements

Prepared statements bring security, efficiency, and convenience. Naturally, it is possible to use them with the Go standard library; this recipe will show how.

Getting ready

Verify if Go is properly installed by calling the `go version` command in your Terminal. If the command fails, follow the *Getting ready* section in the first recipe of this chapter.

Set up the PostgreSQL server, as mentioned in the first recipe of this chapter.

How to do it...

1. Run the following SQL script against your sample database:

```sql
DROP TABLE IF EXISTS post;
CREATE TABLE post (
    ID serial,
    TITLE varchar(40),
    CONTENT varchar(255),
    CONSTRAINT pk_post PRIMARY KEY(ID)
);
SELECT * FROM post;
```

2. Open the console and create the folder `chapter08/recipe04`.

3. Navigate to the directory.

4. Create the `prepared.go` file with the following content:

```go
package main

import (
    "database/sql"
    "fmt"
    _ "github.com/lib/pq"
)

const trunc = "TRUNCATE TABLE post;"
const ins = "INSERT INTO post(ID,TITLE,CONTENT)
              VALUES ($1,$2,$3)"

var testTable = []struct {
    ID int
    Title string
    Content string
}{
    {1, "Title One", "Content of title one"},
    {2, "Title Two", "Content of title two"},
    {3, "Title Three", "Content of title three"},
}

func main() {
    db := createConnection()
    defer db.Close()

    // Truncate table
    _, err := db.Exec(trunc)
    if err != nil {
```

```
    panic(err)
  }

  stm, err := db.Prepare(ins)
  if err != nil {
    panic(err)
  }

  inserted := int64(0)
  for _, val := range testTable {
    fmt.Printf("Inserting record ID: %d\n", val.ID)
    // Execute the prepared statement
    r, err := stm.Exec(val.ID, val.Title, val.Content)
    if err != nil {
      fmt.Printf("Cannot insert record ID : %d\n",
                 val.ID)
    }
    if affected, err := r.RowsAffected(); err == nil {
      inserted = inserted + affected
    }
  }

  fmt.Printf("Result: Inserted %d rows.\n", inserted)

}

func createConnection() *sql.DB {
  connStr := "postgres://postgres:postgres@
              localhost:5432/example?sslmode=disable"
  db, err := sql.Open("postgres", connStr)
  if err != nil {
    panic(err)
  }
  err = db.Ping()
  if err != nil {
    panic(err)
  }
  return db
}
```

5. Execute the code by `go run prepared.go`.

6. See the output:

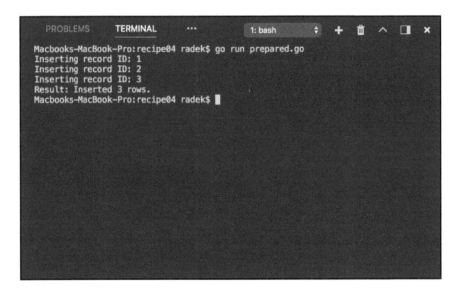

How it works...

To create the prepared statement, the Prepare method of the pointer to the DB struct needs to be called. After this, the Exec or Query method on the Stmt pointer is called with given parameters for the statement.

The prepared statement is created within the scope of the DB pointer, but on the specific connection from the connection pool. The statement remembers which connection has been used, and when it is invoked, it tries to use the same connection. If the connection is busy or was closed, then it recreates the prepared statement and calls the statement on a new connection.

The situation changes if you use the prepared statement within an opened transaction *Tx, in this case, the prepared statement is bound to one connection which is related to the transaction.

Note that prepared statements prepared within the transaction cannot be used with the DB pointer, and vice versa.

In general, the prepared statement works the way the statement is created on the database side. The database returns the identifier of the prepared statement. The prepared statement is executed during the following call, and only the parameters for the statement are provided.

Canceling the pending query

In some cases, you need to prune long running statements to limit the consumption of resources, or just if the result is not relevant, or if the statement is running too long. Since Go 1.8, the canceling of queries is possible. This recipe explains how to use this feature.

Getting ready

Verify if Go is properly installed by calling the `go version` command in your Terminal. If the command fails, follow the *Getting ready* section in the first recipe of this chapter.

Set up the PostgreSQL server, as mentioned in the first recipe of this chapter.

How to do it...

1. Run the following SQL script against your sample database:

```
DROP TABLE IF EXISTS post;
CREATE TABLE post (
  ID serial,
  TITLE varchar(40),
  CONTENT varchar(255),
  CONSTRAINT pk_post PRIMARY KEY(ID)
);
SELECT * FROM post;
INSERT INTO post(ID,TITLE,CONTENT) VALUES
                (1,'Title One','Content One'),
                (2,'Title Two','Content Two');
```

2. Open the console and create the folder `chapter08/recipe05`.
3. Navigate to the directory.

4. Create the `cancelable.go` file with the following content:

```go
package main

import (
  "context"
  "database/sql"
  "fmt"
  "time"
  _ "github.com/lib/pq"
)

const sel = "SELECT * FROM post p CROSS JOIN
    (SELECT 1 FROM generate_series(1,1000000)) tbl"

func main() {
  db := createConnection()
  defer db.Close()

  ctx, canc := context.WithTimeout(context.Background(),
                                   20*time.Microsecond)
  rows, err := db.QueryContext(ctx, sel)
  canc() //cancel the query
  if err != nil {
    fmt.Println(err)
    return
  }
  defer rows.Close()
  count := 0
  for rows.Next() {
    if rows.Err() != nil {
      fmt.Println(rows.Err())
      continue
    }
    count++
  }

  fmt.Printf("%d rows returned\n", count)

}

func createConnection() *sql.DB {
  connStr := "postgres://postgres:postgres@
              localhost:5432/example?sslmode=disable"
  db, err := sql.Open("postgres", connStr)
  if err != nil {
    panic(err)
```

```
  }
  err = db.Ping()
  if err != nil {
    panic(err)
  }
  return db
}
```

5. Execute the code by `go run cancelable.go`.

6. See the output:

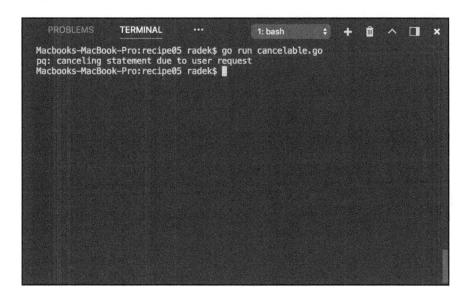

How it works...

The `database/sql` package provides the possibility of canceling the pending statement. All the methods named `XXXContext` of `DB` struct pointer are the ones that consume the context, and it is possible to cancel the pending statement.

The canceling of the statement is possible only if the driver supports the `Context` variant. If it doesn't, the variant without the `Context` is executed.

With the `Context` variant and `context.WithTimeout`, you can create a timeout of the statement call.

Note that the sample code execution ends with the error `pq: canceling statement due to user request`, which corresponds with that of `CancelFunc`, which was called right after the query was executed.

Reading query result metadata

Besides the data itself, the result of a query contains metadata related to the result set. This contains information about the column names, types, and other information about the data. This recipe will explain how to retrieve the data.

Getting ready

Verify if Go is properly installed by calling the `go version` command in your Terminal. If the command fails, follow the *Getting ready* section in the first recipe of this chapter.

Set up the PostgreSQL server, as mentioned in the first recipe of this chapter.

How to do it...

1. Run the following SQL script against your sample database:

```
DROP TABLE IF EXISTS post;
CREATE TABLE post (
  ID serial,
  TITLE varchar(40),
  CONTENT varchar(255),
  CONSTRAINT pk_post PRIMARY KEY(ID)
);
SELECT * FROM post;
INSERT INTO post(ID,TITLE,CONTENT) VALUES
                (1,'Title One','Content One'),
                (2,'Title Two','Content Two');
```

2. Open the console and create the folder `chapter08/recipe06`.
3. Navigate to the directory.

4. Create the `metadata.go` file with the following content:

```go
package main

import (
  "database/sql"
  "fmt"
  _ "github.com/lib/pq"
)

const sel = "SELECT * FROM post p"

func main() {

  db := createConnection()
  defer db.Close()

  rs, err := db.Query(sel)
  if err != nil {
    panic(err)
  }
  defer rs.Close()
  columns, err := rs.Columns()
  if err != nil {
    panic(err)
  }
  fmt.Printf("Selected columns: %v\n", columns)

  colTypes, err := rs.ColumnTypes()
  if err != nil {
    panic(err)
  }
  for _, col := range colTypes {
    fmt.Println()
    fmt.Printf("%+v\n", col)
  }

}

func createConnection() *sql.DB {
  connStr := "postgres://postgres:postgres@
              localhost:5432/example?sslmode=disable"
  db, err := sql.Open("postgres", connStr)
  if err != nil {
    panic(err)
  }
  err = db.Ping()
```

```
      if err != nil {
        panic(err)
      }
      return db
    }
```

5. Execute the code by `go run metadata.go`.

6. See the output:

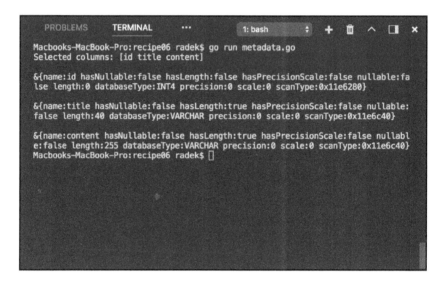

How it works...

The `Query` and `QueryContext` methods of the pointer to the `DB` struct result in the `Rows` struct pointer. The `Rows` pointer provides the methods `Columns` and `ColumnTypes`, which contain the information about the structure of the returned result set.

The `Columns` method returns just the slice of strings with column names.

The `ColumnTypes` method returns the slice of `ColumnType` pointers, which contains more rich information about the returned result set. The preceding code prints out the detailed information of what information the `ColumnType` pointer exposes.

Retrieving data from a query result

While working with the database, the basic part is the extraction of data through executed query. This recipe will illustrate how it is done when using the standard library `database/sql` package.

Getting ready

Verify if Go is properly installed by calling the `go version` command in your Terminal. If the command fails, follow the *Getting ready* section in the first recipe of this chapter.

Set up the PostgreSQL server, as mentioned in the first recipe of this chapter.

How to do it...

1. Run the following SQL script against your sample database:

```sql
DROP TABLE IF EXISTS post;
CREATE TABLE post (
  ID serial,
  TITLE varchar(40),
  CONTENT varchar(255),
  CONSTRAINT pk_post PRIMARY KEY(ID)
);
SELECT * FROM post;
INSERT INTO post(ID,TITLE,CONTENT) VALUES
                (1,'Title One','Content One'),
                (2,NULL,'Content Two');
```

2. Open the console and create the folder `chapter08/recipe07`.
3. Navigate to the directory.
4. Create the `data.go` file with the following content:

```go
package main

import (
  "database/sql"
  "fmt"
  _ "github.com/lib/pq"
)
```

```
const sel = `SELECT title,content FROM post;
SELECT 1234 NUM; `

const selOne = "SELECT title,content FROM post
                WHERE ID = $1;"

type Post struct {
  Name sql.NullString
  Text sql.NullString
}

func main() {
  db := createConnection()
  defer db.Close()

  rs, err := db.Query(sel)
  if err != nil {
    panic(err)
  }
  defer rs.Close()

  posts := []Post{}
  for rs.Next() {
    if rs.Err() != nil {
      panic(rs.Err())
    }
    p := Post{}
    if err := rs.Scan(&p.Name, &p.Text); err != nil {
      panic(err)
    }
    posts = append(posts, p)
  }

  var num int
  if rs.NextResultSet() {
    for rs.Next() {
      if rs.Err() != nil {
        panic(rs.Err())
      }
      rs.Scan(&num)
    }
  }

  fmt.Printf("Retrieved posts: %+v\n", posts)
  fmt.Printf("Retrieved number: %d\n", num)

  row := db.QueryRow(selOne, 100)
  or := Post{}
```

```
  if err := row.Scan(&or.Name, &or.Text); err != nil {
    fmt.Printf("Error: %s\n", err.Error())
    return
  }

  fmt.Printf("Retrieved one post: %+v\n", or)

}

func createConnection() *sql.DB {
  connStr := "postgres://postgres:postgres@
            localhost:5432/example?sslmode=disable"
  db, err := sql.Open("postgres", connStr)
  if err != nil {
    panic(err)
  }
  err = db.Ping()
  if err != nil {
    panic(err)
  }
  return db
}
```

5. Execute the code by `go run data.go`.

6. See the output:

How it works...

The pointer to `Rows` coming from the `Query` method of the pointer to the `DB` struct provides the methods to read and extract the data from the result set.

Note that first the `Next` method should be called to shift the cursor to the next result row. The `Next` method returns `true` if there is any other row, or `false` if not.

After the new row is fetched by `Next`, the `Scan` method could be called to extract the data into a variable. The number of variables must match the number of columns in `SELECT`, otherwise, the `Scan` method is not able to extract the data.

The important part of the code is that, after each `Next` method, the `Err` method should be called to find out if there was an error during the reading of the next row.

The preceding example intentionally uses the `NULL` value for the second record. The `NULL` database values could not be extracted to not nullable types, `string`, in this case, the `NullString` type must be used.

For completeness, the sample code covers the `QueryRow` method, which slightly differs from the `Query` method. This one returns a pointer to the `Row` struct which provides only the `Scan` method. Note, the fact that there are no rows could only be detected after the `Scan` method is called.

Parsing the query result into a map

Sometimes the result of the query or the structure of the table is not clear, and the result needs to be extracted to some flexible structure. This brings us to this recipe, where the extraction of values mapped to column names will be presented.

Getting ready

Verify if Go is properly installed by calling the `go version` command in your Terminal. If the command fails, follow the *Getting ready* section in the first recipe of this chapter.

Set up the PostgreSQL server, as mentioned in the first recipe of this chapter.

How to do it...

1. Run the following SQL script against your sample database:

```
DROP TABLE IF EXISTS post;
CREATE TABLE post (
  ID serial,
  TITLE varchar(40),
  CONTENT varchar(255),
  CONSTRAINT pk_post PRIMARY KEY(ID)
);
SELECT * FROM post;
INSERT INTO post(ID,TITLE,CONTENT) VALUES
                (1,NULL,'Content One'),
                (2,'Title Two','Content Two');
```

2. Open the console and create the folder chapter08/recipe08.
3. Navigate to the directory.
4. Create the querymap.go file with the following content:

```
package main

import (
  "database/sql"
  "fmt"
  _ "github.com/lib/pq"
)

const selOne = "SELECT id,title,content FROM post
                WHERE ID = $1;"

func main() {
  db := createConnection()
  defer db.Close()

  rows, err := db.Query(selOne, 1)
  if err != nil {
    panic(err)
  }
  cols, _ := rows.Columns()
  for rows.Next() {
    m := parseWithRawBytes(rows, cols)
    fmt.Println(m)
    m = parseToMap(rows, cols)
    fmt.Println(m)
  }
```

```
}

func parseWithRawBytes(rows *sql.Rows, cols []string)
                      map[string]interface{} {
  vals := make([]sql.RawBytes, len(cols))
  scanArgs := make([]interface{}, len(vals))
  for i := range vals {
    scanArgs[i] = &vals[i]
  }
  if err := rows.Scan(scanArgs...); err != nil {
    panic(err)
  }
  m := make(map[string]interface{})
  for i, col := range vals {
    if col == nil {
      m[cols[i]] = nil
    } else {
      m[cols[i]] = string(col)
    }
  }
  return m
}

func parseToMap(rows *sql.Rows, cols []string)
              map[string]interface{} {
  values := make([]interface{}, len(cols))
  pointers := make([]interface{}, len(cols))
  for i := range values {
    pointers[i] = &values[i]
  }

  if err := rows.Scan(pointers...); err != nil {
    panic(err)
  }

  m := make(map[string]interface{})
  for i, colName := range cols {
    if values[i] == nil {
      m[colName] = nil
    } else {
      m[colName] = values[i]
    }
  }
  return m
}

func createConnection() *sql.DB {
  connStr := "postgres://postgres:postgres@
```

```
                    localhost:5432/example?sslmode=disable"
    db, err := sql.Open("postgres", connStr)
    if err != nil {
      panic(err)
    }
    err = db.Ping()
    if err != nil {
      panic(err)
    }
    return db
}
```

5. Execute the code by `go run querymap.go`.

6. See the output:

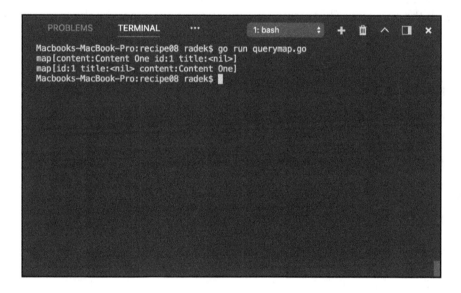

How it works...

Note that the preceding code represents two approaches. The `parseWithRawBytes` function uses the preferred approach, but it is highly dependent on the driver implementation. It works the way that the slice of `RawBytes`, with the same length as the number of the columns in the result, is created. Because the `Scan` function requires pointers to values, we need to create the slice of pointers to the slice of `RawBytes` (slice of byte slices), then it can be passed to the `Scan` function.

After it is successfully extracted, we just remap the values. In the example code, we cast it to the `string` because the driver uses the `string` type to store the values if the `RawBytes` is the target. Beware that the form of stored values depends on driver implementation.

The second approach, `parseToMap`, is usable in the case that the first one does not work. It uses almost the same approach, but the slice of values is defined as the slice of empty interfaces. This approach relies on the driver. The driver should determine the default type to assign to the value pointer.

Handling transactions

Transaction control comes under the common things that need to be kept in mind while working with the database. This recipe will show you how to handle the transaction with the help of the `sql` package.

Getting ready

Verify if Go is properly installed by calling the `go version` command in your Terminal. If the command fails, follow the *Getting ready* section in the first recipe of this chapter.

Set up the PostgreSQL server, as mentioned in the first recipe of this chapter.

How to do it...

1. Run the following SQL script against your sample database:

```
DROP TABLE IF EXISTS post;
CREATE TABLE post (
  ID serial,
  TITLE varchar(40),
  CONTENT varchar(255),
  CONSTRAINT pk_post PRIMARY KEY(ID)
);
SELECT * FROM post;
INSERT INTO post(ID,TITLE,CONTENT) VALUES
                (1,'Title One','Content One'),
                (2,NULL,'Content Two');
```

2. Open the console and create the folder `chapter08/recipe09`.

3. Navigate to the directory.

4. Create the `transaction.go` file with the following content:

```
package main

import (
  "database/sql"
  "fmt"
  _ "github.com/lib/pq"
)

const selOne = "SELECT id,title,content FROM post
                WHERE ID = $1;"
const insert = "INSERT INTO post(ID,TITLE,CONTENT)
        VALUES (4,'Transaction Title','Transaction Content');"

type Post struct {
  ID int
  Title string
  Content string
}

func main() {
  db := createConnection()
  defer db.Close()

  tx, err := db.Begin()
  if err != nil {
    panic(err)
  }
  _, err = tx.Exec(insert)
  if err != nil {
    panic(err)
  }
  p := Post{}
  // Query in other session/transaction
  if err := db.QueryRow(selOne, 4).Scan(&p.ID,
        &p.Title, &p.Content); err != nil {
    fmt.Println("Got error for db.Query:" + err.Error())
  }
  fmt.Println(p)
  // Query within transaction
  if err := tx.QueryRow(selOne, 4).Scan(&p.ID,
        &p.Title, &p.Content); err != nil {
    fmt.Println("Got error for db.Query:" + err.Error())
  }
  fmt.Println(p)
```

```
        // After commit or rollback the
        // transaction need to recreated.
        tx.Rollback()

    }

    func createConnection() *sql.DB {
        connStr := "postgres://postgres:postgres@
                    localhost:5432/example?sslmode=disable"
        db, err := sql.Open("postgres", connStr)
        if err != nil {
            panic(err)
        }
        err = db.Ping()
        if err != nil {
            panic(err)
        }
        return db
    }
```

5. Execute the code by `go run transaction.go`.
6. See the output:

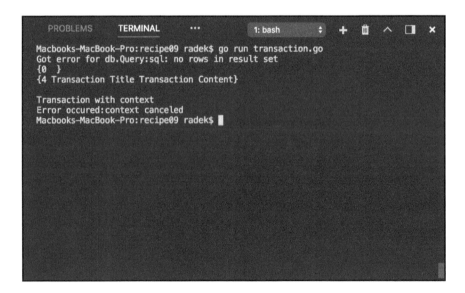

How it works...

The transaction handling, as the preceding code illustrates, is very simple. The method, Begin, of the DB struct pointer creates the transaction with a default isolation level (depends on driver). The transaction, by its nature, is kept on the single connection and is represented by the returned pointer to the Tx struct.

The pointer, Tx, implements all the methods available to the DB struct pointer; the exception is that all the operations are done within the transaction (if the database is able to process the statement in the transaction). The transaction is ended by calling the Rollback or Commit method on the Tx struct pointer. After this call, the transaction is finished and other operations will end by the error ErrTxDone.

There is one more useful method on the DB struct pointer called BeginTx, which creates the transaction Tx struct pointer but is also enhanced with given context. If the context is canceled, the transaction will be rolled back (a further Commit call will result in the error). The BeginTx also consumes the pointer to TxOptions, which is optional and could define the isolation level.

Executing stored procedures and functions

Dealing with stored procedures and functions is always more complex than usual statements, especially if the procedures contain custom types. The standard library provides the API to deal with these, but the final word of how much the stored procedure calls are supported is in the driver implementation. This recipe will show a very simple function/procedure call.

Getting ready

Verify if Go is properly installed by calling the go version command in your Terminal. If the command fails, follow the *Getting ready* section in the first recipe of this chapter.

Set up the PostgreSQL server, as mentioned in the first recipe of this chapter.

How to do it...

1. Run the following SQL script against your sample database:

```
CREATE OR REPLACE FUNCTION format_name
(firstname Text,lastname Text,age INT) RETURNS
VARCHAR AS $$
BEGIN
   RETURN trim(firstname) ||' '||trim(lastname) ||' ('||age||')';
END;
$$ LANGUAGE plpgsql;
```

2. Open the console and create the folder `chapter08/recipe10`.
3. Navigate to the directory.
4. Create the `procedure.go` file with the following content:

```go
package main

import (
  "database/sql"
  "fmt"

  _ "github.com/go-sql-driver/mysql"
  _ "github.com/lib/pq"
)

const call = "select * from format_name($1,$2,$3)"

const callMySQL = "CALL simpleproc(?)"

type Result struct {
  Name string
  Category int
}

func main() {
  db := createConnection()
  defer db.Close()
  r := Result{}

  if err := db.QueryRow(call, "John", "Doe",
              32).Scan(&r.Name); err != nil {
    panic(err)
  }
  fmt.Printf("Result is: %+v\n", r)
}
```

```go
func createConnection() *sql.DB {
  connStr := "postgres://postgres:postgres@localhost:5432
              /example?sslmode=disable"
  db, err := sql.Open("postgres", connStr)
  if err != nil {
    panic(err)
  }
  err = db.Ping()
  if err != nil {
    panic(err)
  }
  return db
}
```

5. Execute the code by `go run procedure.go`.
6. See the output:

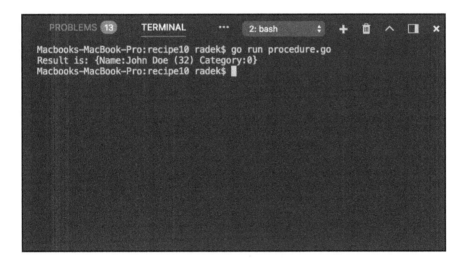

How it works...

The calling of stored procedures is highly dependent on the driver and the database. Note that retrieving result on PostgreSQL database is very similar to querying tables. The `Query` or `QueryRow` method of the `DB` struct pointer is called, and the resulted rows or row pointer can be parsed to obtain the values.

The MySQL driver uses the CALL statement, if the stored procedure needs to be called.

The general problem for almost all drivers ia the OUTPUT parameters of stored procedures. Go 1.9 added support for such parameters, but the majority of drivers of commonly-used databases do not implement this yet. The solution, then, could be the usage of the driver with a nonstandard API.

The way the OUTPUT params are supposed to work is that the procedure call will use the type NamedArg parameter from the Named function of the database/sql package. The Value field of the NamedArg struct should be of type Out which contains the Dest field, where the actual value of the OUTPUT parameter should be placed.

9
Come to the Server Side

This chapter contains the following recipes:

- Creating the TCP server
- Creating the UDP server
- Handling multiple clients
- Creating the HTTP server
- Handling HTTP requests
- Creating HTTP middleware layer
- Serving static files
- Serving content generated with templates
- Handling redirects
- Handling cookies
- Gracefully shutdown the HTTP server
- Serving secured HTTP content
- Resolving form variables

Introduction

This chapter covers topics from implementing simple TCP and UDP servers to spinning the HTTP server. The recipes will lead you from the HTTP request handling, serving the static content, to providing the secured HTTP content.

Check if Go is properly installed. The *Getting ready* section in the *Retrieving Golang version* recipe of Chapter 1, *Interacting With Environment*, will help you.

Make sure the ports 8080 and 7070 are not used by another application.

Creating the TCP server

In the chapter *Connect the Network,* the client side of the TCP connection is presented. In this recipe, the server side will be described.

How to do it...

1. Open the console and create the folder chapter09/recipe01.
2. Navigate to the directory.
3. Create the servertcp.go file with the following content:

```go
package main

import (
  "bufio"
  "fmt"
  "io"
  "net"
)

func main() {

  l, err := net.Listen("tcp", ":8080")
  if err != nil {
    panic(err)
  }
  for {
    fmt.Println("Waiting for client...")
    conn, err := l.Accept()
    if err != nil {
      panic(err)
    }

    msg, err := bufio.NewReader(conn).ReadString('\n')
    if err != nil {
```

```
        panic(err)
      }
      _, err = io.WriteString(conn, "Received: "+string(msg))
      if err != nil {
        fmt.Println(err)
      }
      conn.Close()
    }
}
```

4. Execute the code by `go run servertcp.go`:

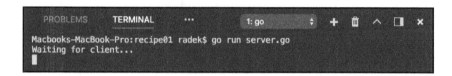

5. Open another Terminal and execute `nc localhost 8080`.

6. Write any text, for example, `Hello`.

7. See the output:

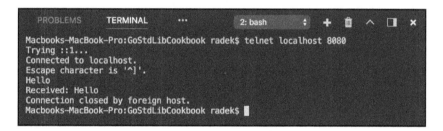

How it works...

The TCP server could be created using the `net` package. The net package contains the `Listen` function that creates the `TCPListener`, which can `Accept` the client connections. The `Accept` method calls on the `TCPListener` blocks until the client connection is received. If the client connection comes, the `Accept` method returns the `TCPConn` connection. The `TCPConn` is a connection to the client that serves to read and write data.

The `TCPConn` implements the `Reader` and `Writer` interfaces. All the approaches to write and read the data could be used. Note that there is a delimiter character for reading the data, otherwise, the EOF is received if the client forcibly closes the connection.

Note that this implementation handles only one client at a time.

Creating the UDP server

The **User Datagram Protocol** (**UDP**) is one of the essential protocols of the internet. This recipe will show you how to listen for the UDP packets and read the content.

How to do it...

1. Open the console and create the folder `chapter09/recipe02`.
2. Navigate to the directory.
3. Create the `serverudp.go` file with the following content:

```
package main

import (
  "fmt"
  "log"
  "net"
)

func main() {

  pc, err := net.ListenPacket("udp", ":7070")
  if err != nil {
    log.Fatal(err)
  }
  defer pc.Close()

  buffer := make([]byte, 2048)
  fmt.Println("Waiting for client...")
  for {
    _, addr, err := pc.ReadFrom(buffer)
    if err == nil {
      rcvMsg := string(buffer)
      fmt.Println("Received: " + rcvMsg)
      if _, err := pc.WriteTo([]byte("Received: "+rcvMsg), addr);
```

```
    err != nil {
        fmt.Println("error on write: " + err.Error())
      }
    } else {
      fmt.Println("error: " + err.Error())
    }
  }
}
```

4. Start the server by `go run serverudp.go`:

5. Open another Terminal and execute `nc -u localhost 7070`.
6. Write any message to the Terminal, for example, `Hello`, and hit *Enter*.
7. See the output:

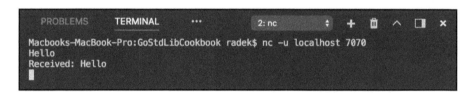

How it works...

As with the TCP server, the UDP server can be created with the help of the `net` package. With the use of the `ListenPacket` function, the `PacketConn` is created.

The `PacketConn` does not implement the `Reader` and `Writer` interface as the `TCPConn`. For reading the received packet, the `ReadFrom` method should be used. The `ReadFrom` method blocks until the packet is received. After this, the `Addr` of the client is returned (remember the UDP is not connection-based). To respond to the client, the `WriteTo` method of `PacketConn` could be used; this consumes the message and the `Addr`, which is the client `Addr`, in this case.

Handling multiple clients

The previous recipes show how to create UDP and TCP servers. The sample codes are not ready to handle multiple clients simultaneously. In this recipe, we will cover how to handle more clients at any given time.

How to do it...

1. Open the console and create the folder `chapter09/recipe03`.
2. Navigate to the directory.
3. Create the `multipletcp.go` file with the following content:

```go
package main

import (
  "fmt"
  "log"
  "net"
)

func main() {

  pc, err := net.ListenPacket("udp", ":7070")
  if err != nil {
    log.Fatal(err)
  }
  defer pc.Close()

  buffer := make([]byte, 2048)
  fmt.Println("Waiting for client...")
  for {

    _, addr, err := pc.ReadFrom(buffer)
    if err == nil {
      rcvMsq := string(buffer)
      fmt.Println("Received: " + rcvMsq)
      if _, err := pc.WriteTo([]byte("Received: "+rcvMsq), addr);
      err != nil {
        fmt.Println("error on write: " + err.Error())
      }
    } else {
      fmt.Println("error: " + err.Error())
    }
```

```
        }

    }
```

4. Execute the code by `go run multipletcp.go`.

5. Open two another Terminals and execute the `nc localhost 8080`.

6. Write something to both opened Terminals and see the output. The following two images are the connected clients.

- Terminal 1 connected to `localhost:8080`:

```
PROBLEMS    TERMINAL    ...         2: nc        +  🗑  ∧  ☐  ✕
Macbooks-MacBook-Pro:GoStdLibCookbook radek$ nc localhost 8080
Welcome client ID: 0
Hello from client 1
Received: Hello from client 1
```

- Terminal 2 connected to `localhost:8080`:

```
PROBLEMS    TERMINAL    ...         3: nc        +  🗑  ∧  ☐  ✕
Macbooks-MacBook-Pro:recipe01 radek$ nc localhost 8080
Welcome client ID: 1
Hello from client 2
Received: Hello from client 2
```

The output in the Terminal where the server is running:

```
PROBLEMS    TERMINAL    ...         1: go        +  🗑  ∧  ☐  ✕
Macbooks-MacBook-Pro:recipe03 radek$ go run multipletcp.go
Waiting for client...
Client ID: 0 connected.
Waiting for client...
Client ID: 1 connected.
Waiting for client...
```

How it works...

The TCP server implementation works the same as the previous recipe, *Creating the TCP server,* from this chapter. The implementation is enhanced, with the ability to handle multiple clients simultaneously. Note that we are now handling the accepted connection in the separate `goroutine`. This means the server can continue to accept the client connections with the `Accept` method.

 Because the UDP protocol is not stateful and does not keep any connection, the handling of multiple clients is moved to application logic and you need to identify the clients and packet sequence. Only the writing response to a client could be parallelized with the use of goroutines.

Creating the HTTP Server

The creation of the HTTP server in Go is very easy, and the standard library provides more ways of how to do that. Let's look at the very basic one.

How to do it...

1. Open the console and create the folder `chapter09/recipe04`.
2. Navigate to the directory.
3. Create the `httpserver.go` file with the following content:

```go
package main

import (
  "fmt"
  "net/http"
)

type SimpleHTTP struct{}

func (s SimpleHTTP) ServeHTTP(rw http.ResponseWriter,
                r *http.Request) {
  fmt.Fprintln(rw, "Hello world")
}

func main() {
  fmt.Println("Starting HTTP server on port 8080")
```

```
    // Eventually you can use
    // http.ListenAndServe(":8080", SimpleHTTP{})
    s := &http.Server{Addr: ":8080", Handler: SimpleHTTP{}}
    s.ListenAndServe()
}
```

4. Execute the code by `go run httpserver.go`.

5. See the output:

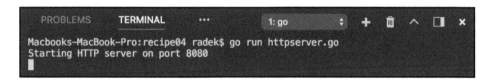

6. Access the URL `http://localhost:8080` in a browser or use `curl`. The `Hello world` content should be displayed:

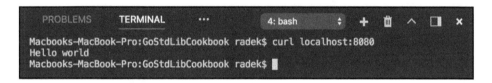

How it works...

The `net/http` package contains a few ways of creating the HTTP server. The most simple one is to implement the `Handler` interface from the `net/http` package. The `Handler` interface requires the type to implement the `ServeHTTP` method. This method handles the request and response.

The server itself is created in the form of the `Server` struct from the `net/http` package. The `Server` struct requires the `Handler` and `Addr` fields. By calling the method, `ListenAndServe`, the server starts serving the content on the given address.

If the `Serve` method of the `Server` is used, then the `Listener` must be provided.

The `net/http` package provides also the default server which could be used if the `ListenAndServe` is called as a function from the `net/http` package. It consumes the `Handler` and `Addr`, the same as the `Server` struct. Internally, the `Server` is created.

Handling HTTP requests

The applications usually use the URL paths and HTTP methods to define the behavior of the application. This recipe will illustrate how to leverage the standard library for handling different URLs and methods.

How to do it...

1. Open the console and create the folder `chapter09/recipe05`.
2. Navigate to the directory.
3. Create the `handle.go` file with the following content:

```go
package main

import (
  "fmt"
  "net/http"
)

func main() {

  mux := http.NewServeMux()
  mux.HandleFunc("/user", func(w http.ResponseWriter,
                 r *http.Request) {
    if r.Method == http.MethodGet {
      fmt.Fprintln(w, "User GET")
    }
    if r.Method == http.MethodPost {
      fmt.Fprintln(w, "User POST")
    }
  })

  // separate handler
  itemMux := http.NewServeMux()
  itemMux.HandleFunc("/items/clothes", func(w http.ResponseWriter,
                     r *http.Request) {
    fmt.Fprintln(w, "Clothes")
  })
  mux.Handle("/items/", itemMux)

  // Admin handlers
  adminMux := http.NewServeMux()
  adminMux.HandleFunc("/ports", func(w http.ResponseWriter,
```

```
                          r *http.Request) {
        fmt.Fprintln(w, "Ports")
    })

    mux.Handle("/admin/", http.StripPrefix("/admin",
                          adminMux))

    // Default server
    http.ListenAndServe(":8080", mux)

}
```

4. Execute the code by `go run handle.go`.
5. Check the following URLs in the browser or via `curl`:
    - `http://localhost:8080/user`
    - `http://localhost:8080/items/clothes`
    - `http://localhost:8080/admin/ports`
6. See the output:

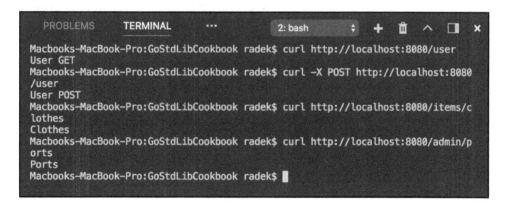

How it works...

The `net/http` package contains the `ServeMux` struct, which implements the `Handler` interface to be used in a `Server` struct, but also contains the mechanism of how to define the handling of different paths. The `ServeMux` pointer contains the methods `HandleFunc` and `Handle`, which accept the path, and the `HandlerFunc` function handles the request for the given path, or another handler does the same.

See the preceding example for how these could be used. The `Handler` interface and `HandlerFunc` require implementing the function with request and response arguments. This way you get access to these two structures. The request itself gives access to `Headers`, the HTTP method, and other request parameters.

Creating HTTP middleware layer

Modern applications with web UI or REST API usually use the middleware mechanism to log the activity, or guard the security of the given interface. In this recipe, the implementation of such a middleware layer will be presented.

How to do it...

1. Open the console and create the folder `chapter09/recipe06`.
2. Navigate to the directory.
3. Create the `middleware.go` file with the following content:

```go
package main

import (
  "io"
  "net/http"
)

func main() {

  // Secured API
  mux := http.NewServeMux()
  mux.HandleFunc("/api/users", Secure(func(w http.ResponseWriter,
               r *http.Request) {
    io.WriteString(w,  `[{"id":"1","login":"ffghi"},
                  {"id":"2","login":"ffghj"}]`)
  }))

  http.ListenAndServe(":8080", mux)

}

func Secure(h http.HandlerFunc) http.HandlerFunc {
  return func(w http.ResponseWriter, r *http.Request) {
    sec := r.Header.Get("X-Auth")
```

```
        if sec != "authenticated" {
          w.WriteHeader(http.StatusUnauthorized)
          return
        }
        h(w, r) // use the handler
      }

   }
```

4. Execute the code by `go run middleware.go`.

5. Check the URL `http://localhost:8080/api/users` with use of `curl` by executing these two commands (the first without and the second with the `X-Auth` header):

   - `curl -X GET -I http://localhost:8080/api/users`
   - `curl -X GET -H "X-Auth: authenticated" -I http://localhost:8080/api/users`

6. See the output:

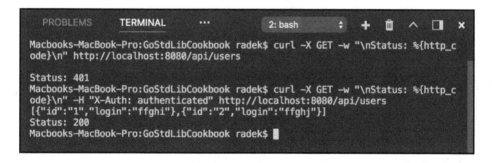

7. Test the URL `http://localhost:8080/api/profile` using the `X-User` header.

8. See the output:

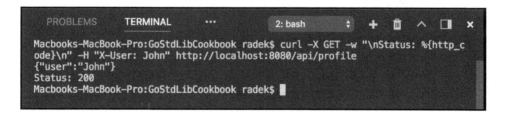

How it works...

The implementation of middleware in the preceding example leverages the *functions as first-class citizens* feature of Golang. The original `HandlerFunc` is wrapped into a `HandlerFunc` which checks the `X-Auth` header. The `Secure` function is then used to secure the `HandlerFunc`, used in the `HandleFunc` methods of `ServeMux`.

Note that this is just a simple example, but this way you can implement more sophisticated solutions. For example, the user identity could be extracted from the `Header` token and subsequently, the new type of handler could be defined as `type AuthHandler func(u *User,w http.ResponseWriter, r *http.Request)`. The function `WithUser` then creates the `HandlerFunc` for the `ServeMux`.

Serving static files

Almost any web application needs to serve static files. The serving of JavaScript files, static HTML pages, or CSS style sheets could be easily achieved with the use of the standard library. This recipe will show how.

How to do it...

1. Open the console and create the folder `chapter09/recipe07`.
2. Navigate to the directory.
3. Create the file `welcome.txt` with the following content:

```
Hi, Go is awesome!
```

4. Create the folder `html`, navigate to it and create the file `page.html` with the following content:

```
<html>
  <body>
    Hi, I'm HTML body for index.html!
  </body>
</html>
```

5. Create the `static.go` file with the following content:

```go
package main

import (
  "net/http"
)

func main() {

    fileSrv := http.FileServer(http.Dir("html"))
    fileSrv = http.StripPrefix("/html", fileSrv)

    http.HandleFunc("/welcome", serveWelcome)
    http.Handle("/html/", fileSrv)
    http.ListenAndServe(":8080", nil)
}

func serveWelcome(w http.ResponseWriter, r *http.Request) {
    http.ServeFile(w, r, "welcome.txt")
}
```

6. Execute the code by `go run static.go`.
7. Check the following URLs with the browser or the `curl` utility:
    * `http://localhost:8080/html/page.html`
    * `http://localhost:8080/welcome`
8. See the output:

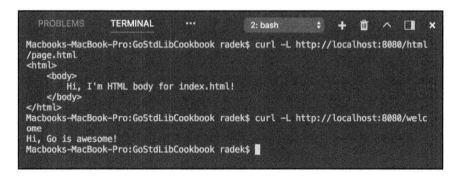

How it works...

The net/http package provides the functions ServeFile and FileServer, which are designed to serve the static files. The ServeFile function just consumes the ResponseWriter and Request with the given file path argument and writes the content of the file to the response.

The FileServer function creates the whole Handler which consumes the FileSystem argument. The preceding example uses the Dir type, which implements the FileSystem interface. The FileSystem interface requires implementing the Open method, which consumes string and returns the actual File for the given path.

Serving content generated with templates

For some purposes, it is not necessary to create highly dynamic web UI with all the JavaScript, and the static content with generated content could be sufficient. The Go standard library provides a way of constructing dynamically generated content. This recipe gives a lead into the Go standard library templating.

How to do it...

1. Open the console and create the folder chapter09/recipe08.
2. Navigate to the directory.
3. Create the file template.tpl with the following content:

```
<html>
  <body>
    Hi, I'm HTML body for index.html!
  </body>
</html>
```

4. Create the file dynamic.go with the following content:

```
package main

import "net/http"
import "html/template"

func main() {
  tpl, err := template.ParseFiles("template.tpl")
```

```
      if err != nil {
        panic(err)
      }

      http.HandleFunc("/",func(w http.ResponseWriter, r *http.Request){
        err := tpl.Execute(w, "John Doe")
        if err != nil {
          panic(err)
        }
      })
      http.ListenAndServe(":8080", nil)
    }
```

5. Execute the code by `go run dynamic.go`.
6. Check the URL `http://localhost:8080` and see the output:

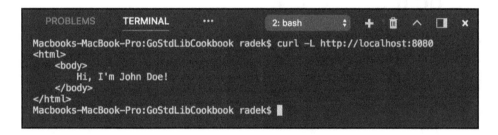

How it works...

The Go standard library also contains the package for templating the content. The packages `html/template` and `text/template` provide the functions to parse the templates and use them to create the output. The parsing is done with the `ParseXXX` functions or the methods of the newly-created `Template` struct pointer. The preceding example uses the `ParseFiles` function of the `html/template` package.

The templates themselves are text-based documents or pieces of text which contain dynamic variables. The use of the template is based on merging the template text with the structure that contains the values for the variables present in the template. For merging the template with such structures, the `Execute` and `ExecuteTemplate` methods are there. Note that these consume the writer interface, where the output is written; the `ResponseWriter` is used in this case.

The template syntax and features are explained well in the documentation.

Handling redirects

Redirects are the usual way of telling the client that the content was moved, or there is a needs to look somewhere else to accomplish the request. This recipe describes the way to implement redirects with the standard library.

How to do it...

1. Open the console and create the folder chapter09/recipe09.
2. Navigate to the directory.
3. Create the file redirect.go with the following content:

```go
package main

import (
  "fmt"
  "log"
  "net/http"
)

func main() {
  log.Println("Server is starting...")

  http.Handle("/secured/handle",
      http.RedirectHandler("/login",
           http.StatusTemporaryRedirect))
  http.HandleFunc("/secured/hadlefunc",
      func(w http.ResponseWriter, r *http.Request) {
    http.Redirect(w, r, "/login", http.StatusTemporaryRedirect)
  })
  http.HandleFunc("/login", func(w http.ResponseWriter,
                 r *http.Request) {
    fmt.Fprintf(w, "Welcome user! Please login!\n")
  })
  if err := http.ListenAndServe(":8080", nil); err != nil {
    panic(err)
```

```
    }
  }
```

4. Execute the code by `go run redirect.go`.

5. Use `curl -v -L http://localhost:8080/secured/handle` to see if redirect works:

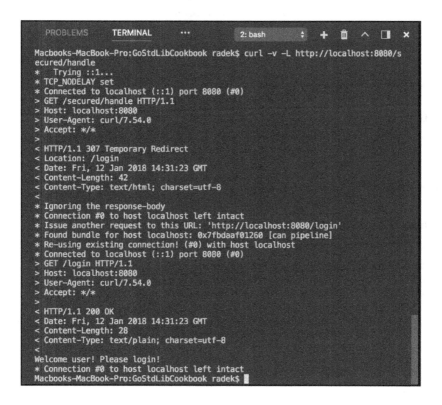

How it works...

The `net/http` package contains a simple way of executing the redirect. The `RedirectHandler` could be utilized. The function consumes the `URL` where the request will be redirected and the `status code` which will be sent to client. The function itself sends results to the `Handler`, which could be used in the `Handle` method of `ServeMux` (the example uses the default one directly from the package).

The second approach is the use of the `Redirect` function, which does the redirect for you. The function consumes `ResponseWriter`, the request pointer and the same as `RequestHandler`, the URL and status code, which will be sent to the client.

 The redirect could be also done with the help of manually setting the `Location` header and writing the proper status code. The Go library only makes this easy to use for the developer.

Handling cookies

Cookies provide a way of easily storing data on the client side. This recipe illustrates how to set, retrieve and remove the cookies with the help of the standard library.

How to do it...

1. Open the console and create the folder `chapter09/recipe10`.
2. Navigate to the directory.
3. Create the file `cookies.go` with the following content:

```go
package main

import (
  "fmt"
  "log"
  "net/http"
  "time"
)

const cookieName = "X-Cookie"

func main() {
  log.Println("Server is starting...")

  http.HandleFunc("/set", func(w http.ResponseWriter,
                  r *http.Request) {
    c := &http.Cookie{
      Name: cookieName,
      Value: "Go is awesome.",
      Expires: time.Now().Add(time.Hour),
      Domain: "localhost",
```

```
        }
        http.SetCookie(w, c)
        fmt.Fprintln(w, "Cookie is set!")
    })
    http.HandleFunc("/get", func(w http.ResponseWriter,
                    r *http.Request) {
        val, err := r.Cookie(cookieName)
        if err != nil {
            fmt.Fprintln(w, "Cookie err: "+err.Error())
            return
        }
        fmt.Fprintf(w, "Cookie is: %s \n", val.Value)
        fmt.Fprintf(w, "Other cookies")
        for _, v := range r.Cookies() {
            fmt.Fprintf(w, "%s => %s \n", v.Name, v.Value)
        }
    })
    http.HandleFunc("/remove", func(w http.ResponseWriter,
                    r *http.Request) {
        val, err := r.Cookie(cookieName)
        if err != nil {
            fmt.Fprintln(w, "Cookie err: "+err.Error())
            return
        }
        val.MaxAge = -1
        http.SetCookie(w, val)
        fmt.Fprintln(w, "Cookie is removed!")
    })
    if err := http.ListenAndServe(":8080", nil); err != nil {
        panic(err)
    }
}
```

4. Execute the code by `go run cookies.go`.

5. Access the URLs in the following sequence and see:

- The response in a browser directed to the URL
  `http://localhost:8080/set`:

- The response in a browser directed to the
  URL `http://localhost:8080/get` (the response contains the
  available cookies):

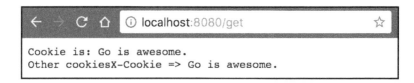

- The response in a browser directed to the
  URL `http://localhost:8080/remove` (this will remove the
  cookie):

- The response in a browser directed to the
  URL `http://localhost:8080/get` (proof that the cookie X-
  Cookie was removed):

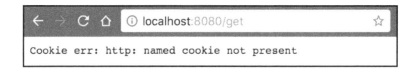

How it works...

The `net/http` package also provides the functions and mechanisms to operate on cookies. The sample code presents how to set/get and remove the cookies. The `SetCookie` function accepts the `Cookie` struct pointer that represents the cookies, and naturally the `ResponseWriter`. The `Name`, `Value`, `Domain`, and expiration are set directly in the `Cookie` struct. Behind the scenes, the `SetCookie` function writes the header to set the cookies.

The cookie values could be retrieved from the `Request` struct. The method `Cookie` with the name parameter returns the pointer to the `Cookie`, if the cookie exists in the request.

To list all cookies within the request, the method `Cookies` could be called. This method returns the slice of the `Cookie` structs pointers.

To let the client know that the cookie should be removed, the `Cookie` with the given name could be retrieved and the `MaxAge` field should be set to a negative value. Note that this is not a Go feature, but the way the client should work.

Gracefully shutdown the HTTP server

In `Chapter 1`, *Interacting with the Environment*, the mechanism of how to implement graceful shutdown was presented. In this recipe, we will describe how to shut down the HTTP server and give it time to handle the existing clients.

How to do it...

1. Open the console and create the folder `chapter09/recipe11`.
2. Navigate to the directory.
3. Create the file `gracefully.go` with the following content:

```go
package main

import (
  "context"
  "fmt"
  "log"
  "net/http"
  "os"
  "os/signal"
  "time"
)

func main() {

  mux := http.NewServeMux()
  mux.HandleFunc("/",func(w http.ResponseWriter, r *http.Request){
    fmt.Fprintln(w, "Hello world!")
  })
```

```
srv := &http.Server{Addr: ":8080", Handler: mux}
go func() {
  if err := srv.ListenAndServe(); err != nil {
    log.Printf("Server error: %s\n", err)
  }
}()

log.Println("Server listening on : " + srv.Addr)

stopChan := make(chan os.Signal)
signal.Notify(stopChan, os.Interrupt)

<-stopChan // wait for SIGINT
log.Println("Shutting down server...")

ctx, cancel := context.WithTimeout(
  context.Background(),
  5*time.Second)
srv.Shutdown(ctx)
<-ctx.Done()
cancel()
log.Println("Server gracefully stopped")
}
```

4. Execute the code by `go run gracefully.go`.

5. Wait until the server starts listening:

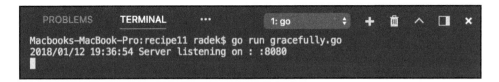

6. Connect with the browser to `http://localhost:8080`; this will cause the browser to wait for a response for 10 seconds.

7. Within the interval of 10 seconds, press *Ctrl + C* to send the `SIGINT` signal.

8. Try to connect again from another tab (the server should refuse other connections).

9. See the output in the Terminal:

```
PROBLEMS    TERMINAL    ...              1: bash    ⬍  +  🗑  ∧  ⬜  ✕
Macbooks-MacBook-Pro:recipe11 radek$ go run gracefully.go
2018/01/12 19:50:17 Server listening on : :8080
^C2018/01/12 19:50:24 Shutting down server...
2018/01/12 19:50:24 Server error: http: Server closed
2018/01/12 19:50:31 Server gracefully stopped
Macbooks-MacBook-Pro:recipe11 radek$ ▮
```

How it works...

The `Server` from the `net/http` package provides the method to gracefully shutdown the connection. The preceding code starts the HTTP server in a separate `goroutine` and keeps the reference to the `Server` struct in a variable.

By calling the `Shutdown` method, the `Server` starts refusing new connections and closes opened listeners and idle connections. Then it waits indefinitely for the already pending connections, till these become idle. After all the connections are closed, the server shuts down. Note that the `Shutdown` method consumes the `Context`. If the provided `Context` expires prior to the shutdown, then the error from `Context` is returned and the `Shutdown` does not block anymore.

Serving secured HTTP content

This recipe describes the simplest way of creating the HTTP server, which serves the content via the TLS/SSL layer.

Getting ready

Prepare the private key and self-signed X-509 certificate. For this purpose, the OpenSSL utility could be used. By executing the command `openssl genrsa -out server.key 2048`, the private key derived with the use of an RSA algorithm is generated to the file `server.key`. Based on this private key, the X-509 certificate could be generated by calling `openssl req -new -x509 -sha256 -key server.key -out server.crt -days 365`. The `server.crt` file is created.

How to do it...

1. Open the console and create the folder `chapter09/recipe12`.
2. Navigate to the directory.
3. Place the created `server.key` and `server.crt` files in it.
4. Create the file `servetls.go` with the following content:

```
package main

import (
  "fmt"
  "net/http"
)

type SimpleHTTP struct{}

func (s SimpleHTTP) ServeHTTP(rw http.ResponseWriter,
                    r *http.Request) {
  fmt.Fprintln(rw, "Hello world")
}

func main() {
  fmt.Println("Starting HTTP server on port 8080")
  // Eventually you can use
  // http.ListenAndServe(":8080", SimpleHTTP{})
  s := &http.Server{Addr: ":8080", Handler: SimpleHTTP{}}
  if err := s.ListenAndServeTLS("server.crt", "server.key");
  err != nil {
    panic(err)
  }
}
```

5. Execute the server by `go run servetls.go`.
6. Access the URL `https://localhost:8080` (the HTTPS protocol is used). If using the `curl` utility, the `--insecure` flag must be used, as our certificate is self-signed and not trusted:

```
PROBLEMS    TERMINAL    ...              2: bash        +   🗑  ^  ☐  ✕

Macbooks-MacBook-Pro:GoStdLibCookbook radek$ curl —insecure https://localhost:
8080
Hello world
Macbooks-MacBook-Pro:GoStdLibCookbook radek$ ▊
```

How it works...

Besides the `ListenAndServe` function, within the `net/http` package, the TLS variant for serving HTTP via SSL/TLS, exists. With the use of the `ListenAndServeTLS` method of the `Server`, the secured HTTP is served. The `ListenAndServeTLS` consumes the path to the private key and X-509 certificate. Naturally, the function `ListenAndServeTLS`, directly from `net/http` package, could be used.

Resolving form variables

The HTTP POST form is a very common way of passing the information to the server, in a structured way. This recipe shows how to parse and access these on the server side.

How to do it...

1. Open the console and create the folder `chapter09/recipe12`.
2. Navigate to the directory.
3. Create the file `form.go` with the following content:

```go
package main

import (
  "fmt"
  "net/http"
)

type StringServer string

func (s StringServer) ServeHTTP(rw http.ResponseWriter,
                     req *http.Request) {
  fmt.Printf("Prior ParseForm: %v\n", req.Form)
  req.ParseForm()
  fmt.Printf("Post ParseForm: %v\n", req.Form)
  fmt.Println("Param1 is : " + req.Form.Get("param1"))
  rw.Write([]byte(string(s)))
}

func createServer(addr string) http.Server {
  return http.Server{
    Addr: addr,
    Handler: StringServer("Hello world"),
```

```go
    }
  }

  func main() {
    s := createServer(":8080")
    fmt.Println("Server is starting...")
    if err := s.ListenAndServe(); err != nil {
      panic(err)
    }
  }
```

4. Execute the code by `go run form.go`.

5. Open the second Terminal and execute the `POST` using `curl`:

```
curl -X POST -H "Content-Type: app
lication/x-www-form-urlencoded" -d "param1=data1&param2=data2"
"localhost:8080?
param1=overriden&param3=data3"
```

6. See the output in the first Terminal, where the server is running:

```
PROBLEMS     TERMINAL    ...          1: go

Macbooks-MacBook-Pro:recipe13 radek$ go run form.go
Server is starting...
Prior ParseForm: map[]
Post ParseForm: map[param1:[data1 overriden] param2:[data2] param3:[data3]]
Param1 is : data1
PostForm : map[param1:[data1] param2:[data2]]
```

How it works...

The `Request` struct of the `net/http` package contains the `Form` field which contains the `POST` form variables and URL query variables merged. The important step in the preceding code is the call of the `ParseForm` method on the `Request` pointer. This method call causes the parsing of the `POST` form values and query values into a `Form` variable. Note that if the `Get` method on the `Form` field is used, the `POST` value of the parameter is prioritized. The `Form` and `PostForm` fields are, in fact, of type `url.Values`.

If only the parameters from the `POST` form need to be accessed, the `PostForm` field of the `Request` is provided. This one keeps only those that were part of the `POST` body.

10
Fun with Concurrency

This chapter contains the following recipes:

- Synchronizing access to a resource with Mutex
- Creating a map for concurrent access
- Running a code block only once
- Pooling resources across multiple goroutines
- Synchronizing goroutines with WaitGroup
- Getting the fastest result from multiple sources
- Propagating errors with errgroup

Introduction

The programming of concurrent behavior is always hard. Go has pretty good mechanisms for managing the concurrency in the form of channels. Besides the channels as a synchronization mechanism, the Go standard library provides the package to handle the concurrent parts of the more traditional core way. This chapter describes how to leverage the sync package for implementing common synchronization tasks. The final recipe will show the simplification of error propagation for a group of goroutines.

Check if Go is properly installed. The *Getting ready* section in the *Retrieving Golang version* recipe of `Chapter 1`, *Interacting with the Environment*, will help you.

Make sure the ports `8080` and `7070` are not used by another application.

Synchronizing access to a resource with Mutex

In case the code uses the concurrent access to any resource which is considered to be unsafe for concurrent use, it is necessary to implement a synchronization mechanism to secure the access. Besides the channel usage, Mutex could be leveraged for this purpose. This recipe will show you how.

How to do it...

1. Open the console and create the folder `chapter10/recipe01`.
2. Navigate to the directory.
3. Create the file `mutex.go` with the following content:

```go
package main

import (
  "fmt"
  "sync"
)

var names = []string{"Alan", "Joe", "Jack", "Ben",
                     "Ellen", "Lisa", "Carl", "Steve",
                     "Anton", "Yo"}

type SyncList struct {
  m sync.Mutex
  slice []interface{}
}

func NewSyncList(cap int) *SyncList {
  return &SyncList{
    sync.Mutex{},
    make([]interface{}, cap),
```

```
    }
  }

  func (l *SyncList) Load(i int) interface{} {
    l.m.Lock()
    defer l.m.Unlock()
    return l.slice[i]
  }

  func (l *SyncList) Append(val interface{}) {
    l.m.Lock()
    defer l.m.Unlock()
    l.slice = append(l.slice, val)
  }

  func (l *SyncList) Store(i int, val interface{}) {
    l.m.Lock()
    defer l.m.Unlock()
    l.slice[i] = val
  }

  func main() {

    l := NewSyncList(0)
    wg := &sync.WaitGroup{}
    wg.Add(10)
    for i := 0; i < 10; i++ {
      go func(idx int) {
        l.Append(names[idx])
        wg.Done()
      }(i)
    }
    wg.Wait()

    for i := 0; i < 10; i++ {
      fmt.Printf("Val: %v stored at idx: %d\n", l.Load(i), i)
    }

  }
```

4. Execute the code by go run mutex.go.

5. See the output:

How it works...

The synchronization primitive Mutex is provided by the package sync. The Mutex works as a lock above the secured section or resource. Once the goroutine calls Lock on the Mutex and the Mutex is in the unlocked state, the Mutex becomes locked and the goroutine gets exclusive access to the critical section. In case the Mutex is in the locked state, the goroutine calls the Lock method. This goroutine is blocked and needs to wait until the Mutex gets unlocked again.

Note that in the example, we use the Mutex to synchronize access on a slice primitive, which is considered to be unsafe for the concurrent use.

The important fact is that the Mutex cannot be copied after its first use.

Creating map for concurrent access

The map primitive in Golang should be considered as unsafe for concurrent access. In the previous recipe, we described how to synchronize access to the resource with Mutex, which could also be leveraged with access to the map primitive. But the Go standard library also provides the map structure designed for concurrent access. This recipe will illustrate how to work with it.

How to do it...

1. Open the console and create the folder `chapter10/recipe02`.
2. Navigate to the directory.
3. Create the file `map.go` with the following content:

```
package main

import (
  "fmt"
  "sync"
)

var names = []string{"Alan", "Joe", "Jack", "Ben",
                     "Ellen", "Lisa", "Carl", "Steve",
                     "Anton", "Yo"}

func main() {

  m := sync.Map{}
  wg := &sync.WaitGroup{}
  wg.Add(10)
  for i := 0; i < 10; i++ {
    go func(idx int) {
      m.Store(fmt.Sprintf("%d", idx), names[idx])
      wg.Done()
    }(i)
  }
  wg.Wait()

  v, ok := m.Load("1")
  if ok {
    fmt.Printf("For Load key: 1 got %v\n", v)
  }

  v, ok = m.LoadOrStore("11", "Tim")
  if !ok {
    fmt.Printf("Key 11 missing stored val: %v\n", v)
  }

  m.Range(func(k, v interface{}) bool {
    key, _ := k.(string)
    t, _ := v.(string)
    fmt.Printf("For index %v got %v\n", key, t)
```

```
        return true
    })

}
```

4. Execute the code by `go run map.go`.
5. See the output:

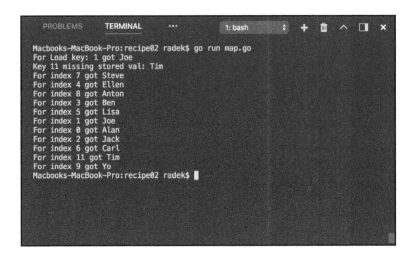

How it works...

The package `sync`, contains the structure `Map` that is designed to be used concurrently from multiple Go routines. The `Map` struct, with its methods, mimics the behavior of the map primitive. The `Store` method is the equivalent of the `m[key] = val` statement. The `Load` method is equal to `val, ok := m[key]` and the `Range` method provides the ability to iterate through the map. Note that the `Range` function works with the current state of `Map`, so if the values are changed during the running `Range` method, the changes are reflected, but only if the key wasn't already visited. The `Range` function visits its keys only once.

Running a code block only once

In situations when multiple goroutines run the same code and there is a code block that initializes, for example, shared resource, the Go standard library offers the solution, which will be described further.

How to do it...

1. Open the console and create the folder `chapter10/recipe03`.
2. Navigate to the directory.
3. Create the file `once.go` with the following content:

```go
package main

import (
  "fmt"
  "sync"
)

var names = []interface{}{"Alan", "Joe", "Jack", "Ben",
                          "Ellen", "Lisa", "Carl", "Steve",
                          "Anton", "Yo"}

type Source struct {
  m *sync.Mutex
  o *sync.Once
  data []interface{}
}

func (s *Source) Pop() (interface{}, error) {
  s.m.Lock()
  defer s.m.Unlock()
  s.o.Do(func() {
    s.data = names
    fmt.Println("Data has been loaded.")
  })
  if len(s.data) > 0 {
    res := s.data[0]
    s.data = s.data[1:]
    return res, nil
  }
  return nil, fmt.Errorf("No data available")
}

func main() {

  s := &Source{&sync.Mutex{}, &sync.Once{}, nil}
  wg := &sync.WaitGroup{}
  wg.Add(10)
  for i := 0; i < 10; i++ {
    go func(idx int) {
      // This code block is done only once
```

```
            if val, err := s.Pop(); err == nil {
                fmt.Printf("Pop %d returned: %s\n", idx, val)
            }
            wg.Done()
        }(i)
    }
    wg.Wait()
}
```

4. Execute the code by `go run once.go`.

5. See the output:

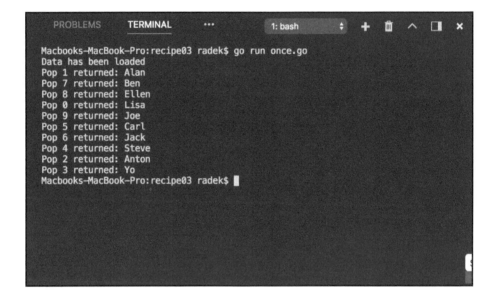

How it works...

The sample code illustrates the lazy loading of the data while accessing the container structure. As the data should be loaded only once, the `Once` struct from the sync package is used in the method `Pop`. The `Once` implements only one method called `Do` which consumes the `func` with no arguments and the function is executed only once per `Once` instance, during the execution.

The `Do` method calls blocks until the first run is done. This fact corresponds with the fact that `Once` is intended to be used for initialization.

Pooling resources across multiple goroutines

Resource pooling is the traditional way to improve performance and save resources. Usually, it is worth pooling the resources with expensive initialization. The Go standard library provides the skeleton structure for a resource pool, which is considered to be safe for multiple goroutines access. This recipe describes how to use it.

How to do it...

1. Open the console and create the folder `chapter10/recipe04`.
2. Navigate to the directory.
3. Create the file `pool.go` with the following content:

```go
package main

import "sync"
import "fmt"
import "time"

type Worker struct {
  id string
}

func (w *Worker) String() string {
  return w.id
}

var globalCounter = 0

var pool = sync.Pool{
  New: func() interface{} {
    res := &Worker{fmt.Sprintf("%d", globalCounter)}
    globalCounter++
    return res
  },
}

func main() {
  wg := &sync.WaitGroup{}
  wg.Add(10)
  for i := 0; i < 10; i++ {
```

```
          go func(idx int) {
            // This code block is done only once
            w := pool.Get().(*Worker)
            fmt.Println("Got worker ID: " + w.String())
            time.Sleep(time.Second)
            pool.Put(w)
            wg.Done()
          }(i)
      }
      wg.Wait()
  }
```

4. Execute the code by `go run pool.go`.

5. See the output:

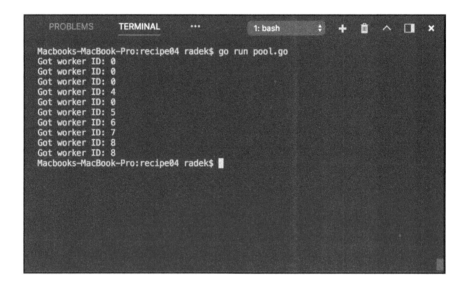

How it works...

The `sync` package contains the struct for pooling the resources. The `Pool` struct has the `Get` and `Put` method to retrieve and put the resource back to the pool. The `Pool` struct is considered to be safe for concurrent access.

While creating the `Pool` struct, the `New` field needs to be set. The `New` field is a no-argument function that should return the pointer to the pooled item. This function is then called in case the new object in the pool needs to be initialized.

Note from the logs of the preceding example, that the `Worker` is reused while returned to the pool. The important fact is that there shouldn't be any assumption related to the retrieved items by `Get` and returned items to `Put` method (like I've put three objects to pool just now, so there will be at least three available). This is mainly caused by the fact that that the idle items in a `Pool` could be automatically removed at any time.

 The pooling of resources is usually worth it if the resource initialization is expensive. Still, the management of resources brings some additional cost.

Synchronizing goroutines with WaitGroup

While working with concurrently running code branches, it is no exception that at some point the program needs to wait for concurrently running parts of the code. This recipe gives insight into how to use the `WaitGroup` to wait for running goroutines.

How to do it...

1. Open the console and create the folder `chapter10/recipe05`.
2. Navigate to the directory.
3. Create the file `syncgroup.go` with the following content:

```go
package main

import "sync"
import "fmt"

func main() {
  wg := &sync.WaitGroup{}
  for i := 0; i < 10; i++ {
    wg.Add(1)
    go func(idx int) {
      // Do some work
      defer wg.Done()
      fmt.Printf("Exiting %d\n", idx)
```

```
            }(i)
        }
        wg.Wait()
        fmt.Println("All done.")
    }
```

4. Execute the code by `go run syncgroup.go`.

5. See the output:

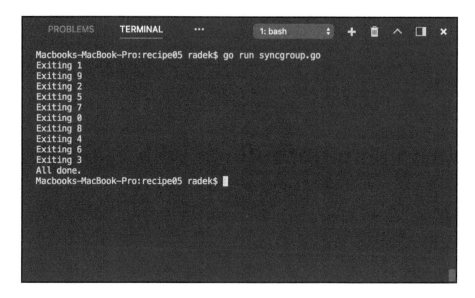

How it works...

With help of the `WaitGroup` struct from the `sync` package, the program run is able to wait until some finite number of goroutines finish. The `WaitGroup` struct implements the method `Add` to add the number of goroutines to wait for. Then after the goroutine finishes, the `Done` method should be called to decrement the number of goroutines to wait for. The method `Wait` is called as a block until the given number of `Done` calls has been done (usually at the end of a `goroutine`). The `WaitGroup` should be used the same way as all synchronization primitives within the sync package. After the creation of the object, the struct should not be copied.

Getting the fastest result from multiple sources

In some cases, for example, while integrating information retrieval from multiple sources, you only need the first result, the fastest one, and the other results are irrelevant after that. An example from the real world could be extracting the currency rate to count the price. You have multiple third-party services and because you need to show the prices as fast as possible, you need only the first rate received from any service. This recipe will show the pattern for how to achieve such behavior.

How to do it...

1. Open the console and create the folder `chapter10/recipe06`.
2. Navigate to the directory.
3. Create the file `first.go` with following content:

```go
package main

import (
  "context"
  "fmt"
  "sync"
  "time"
)

type SearchSrc struct {
  ID string
  Delay int
}

func (s *SearchSrc) Search(ctx context.Context) <-chan string {
  out := make(chan string)
  go func() {
    time.Sleep(time.Duration(s.Delay) * time.Second)
    select {
      case out <- "Result " + s.ID:
      case <-ctx.Done():
      fmt.Println("Search received Done()")
    }
    close(out)
    fmt.Println("Search finished for ID: " + s.ID)
  }()
```

```
    return out
}

func main() {

  ctx, cancel := context.WithCancel(context.Background())

  src1 := &SearchSrc{"1", 2}
  src2 := &SearchSrc{"2", 6}

  r1 := src1.Search(ctx)
  r2 := src2.Search(ctx)

  out := merge(ctx, r1, r2)

  for firstResult := range out {
    cancel()
    fmt.Println("First result is: " + firstResult)
  }
}

func merge(ctx context.Context, results ...<-chan string)
          <-chan string {
  wg := sync.WaitGroup{}
  out := make(chan string)

  output := func(c <-chan string) {
    defer wg.Done()
    select {
      case <-ctx.Done():
        fmt.Println("Received ctx.Done()")
      case res := <-c:
      out <- res
    }
  }

  wg.Add(len(results))
  for _, c := range results {
    go output(c)
  }

  go func() {
    wg.Wait()
    close(out)
  }()
  return out
}
```

4. Execute the code by `go run first.go`.

5. See the output:

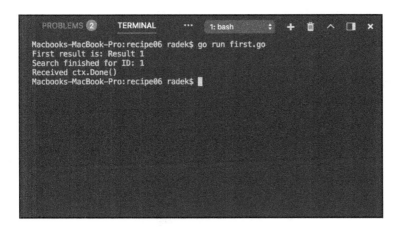

How it works...

The preceding code proposes the solution on executing multiple tasks that output some results, and we need only the first fastest one. The solution uses the `Context` with the cancel function to call cancel once the first result is obtained. The `SearchSrc` structure provides the `Search` method that results in a channel where the result is written. Note that the `Search` method simulates the delay with the `time.Sleep` function. The merge function, for each channel from the `Search` method, triggers the `goroutine` that writes to the final output channel that is read in the `main` method. While the first result is received from the output channel produced from the `merge` function, the `CancelFunc` stored in the variable `cancel` is called to cancel the rest of the processing.

 Be aware that the `Search` method still needs to end, even if its result would not be processed; so this needs to be handled to avoid the `goroutine` and channel leak.

Propagating errors with errgroup

This recipe will show how to easily use the errgroup extension package to detect the error within the group of goroutines that run subtasks, within a common task.

How to do it...

1. Open the console and create the folder `chapter10/recipe07`.
2. Navigate to the directory.
3. Create the file `lines.go` with the following content:

```go
package main

import (
  "bufio"
  "context"
  "fmt"
  "log"
  "strings"

  "golang.org/x/sync/errgroup"
)

const data = `line one
line two with more words
error: This is erroneous line`

func main() {
  log.Printf("Application %s starting.", "Error Detection")
  scanner := bufio.NewScanner(strings.NewReader(data))
  scanner.Split(bufio.ScanLines)

  // For each line fire a goroutine
  g, _ := errgroup.WithContext(context.Background())
  for scanner.Scan() {
    row := scanner.Text()
    g.Go(func() error {
      return func(s string) error {
        if strings.Contains(s, "error:") {
          return fmt.Errorf(s)
        }
        return nil
      }(row)
    })
  }

  // Wait until the goroutines finish
  if err := g.Wait(); err != nil {
```

```
        fmt.Println("Error while waiting: " + err.Error())
    }

}
```

4. Execute the code by `go run lines.go`.
5. See the output:

How it works...

The `golang.org/x/sync/errgroup` package helps to simplify the error propagation and cancellation by context for goroutine groups. The `Group` contains the Go method which consumes the no-arg function returning the `error`. This function should contain the task which should be done by the executed `goroutine`. The `Wait` method of the `Group` from `errgroup` waits until all executed tasks from the Go method are complete, and if any of them are returned `err`, then the first non-nil error is returned. This way, it is possible to simply propagate the error from the group of running goroutines.

Note that the `Group` is also created with the use of context. The `Context` serves as the mechanism to cancel other tasks, if the error occurs. After the `goroutine` function returns the `error`, the inner implementation cancels the context and so could be the running task.

11
Tips and Tricks

This chapter will cover the following recipes:

- Logging customization
- Testing the code
- Benchmarking the code
- Creating subtests
- Testing the HTTP handler
- Accessing tags via reflection
- Sorting slices
- Breaking HTTP handlers into groups
- Utilizing HTTP/2 server push

Introduction

This last chapter adds some additional recipes related to testing, designing your application interface, and leveraging the packages, `sort` and `reflect`.

 Check if Go is properly installed. The *Getting ready* section in the *Retrieving Golang version* recipe of `Chapter 1`, *Interacting with the Environment* will help you.

Make sure the port `8080` is not used by another application.

Logging customization

Besides the logging with the default logger from the `log` package, the standard library also provides a way to create the custom logger, according to the needs of the application or package. This recipe will give a brief insight on how to create one.

How to do it...

1. Open the console and create the folder `chapter11/recipe01`.
2. Navigate to the directory.
3. Create the file `logging.go` with the following content:

```go
package main

import (
  "log"
  "os"
)

func main() {
  custLogger := log.New(os.Stdout, "custom1: ",
                        log.Ldate|log.Ltime)
  custLogger.Println("Hello I'm customized")

  custLoggerEnh := log.New(os.Stdout, "custom2: ",
                           log.Ldate|log.Lshortfile)
  custLoggerEnh.Println("Hello I'm customized logger 2")

}
```

4. Execute the code by `go run logging.go`.
5. See the output:

```
PROBLEMS    TERMINAL    ...          1: bash        +  🗑  ⌃  ▢  ✕

Macbooks-MacBook-Pro:recipe01 radek$ go run logging.go
custom1: 2018/01/17 18:09:31 Hello I'm customized
custom2: 2018/01/17 logging.go:13: Hello I'm customized logger 2
Macbooks-MacBook-Pro:recipe01 radek$ ▊
```

How it works...

The `log` package provides the `New` function which simplifies the creation of a customized logger. The `New` function consumes the `Writer`, which could be any object implementing the `Writer` interface, the prefix in the form of the string, and the form of the logged message that is composed of flags. The last argument is the most interesting because with it, you are able to enhance the log message with dynamic fields, such as date and filename.

Note that the preceding example uses, for the first logger, the `custLogger`, the flags configuring the message to display the date and time in front of the log message. The second one, named the `custLoggerEnh`, uses the flag, `Ldate` and `Lshortfile`, to show the filename and date.

Testing the code

Testing and benchmarking naturally belong to software development. Go, as a modern language with its built-in libraries, supports these from scratch. In this recipe, the basics of testing will be described.

How to do it...

1. Open the console and create the folder `chapter11/recipe02`.
2. Navigate to the directory.
3. Create the file `sample_test.go` with the following content:

```
package main

import (
  "strconv"
  "testing"
)

func TestSampleOne(t *testing.T) {
  expected := "11"
  result := strconv.Itoa(10)
  compare(expected, result, t)
}

func TestSampleTwo(t *testing.T) {
  expected := "11"
```

```
    result := strconv.Itoa(10)
    compareWithHelper(expected, result, t)
}

func TestSampleThree(t *testing.T) {
  expected := "10"
  result := strconv.Itoa(10)
  compare(expected, result, t)
}

func compareWithHelper(expected, result string, t *testing.T) {
  t.Helper()
  if expected != result {
    t.Fatalf("Expected result %v does not match result %v",
        expected, result)
  }
}

func compare(expected, result string, t *testing.T) {
  if expected != result {
    t.Fatalf("Fail: Expected result %v does not match result %v",
        expected, result)
  }
  t.Logf("OK: Expected result %v = %v",
      expected, result)
}
```

4. Execute the test by `go test -v`.

5. See the output in the Terminal:

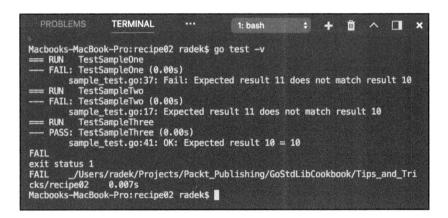

How it works...

The `testing` package of the standard library provides support for the code testing needs. The `test` function needs to fulfill the name pattern, `TestXXX`. By default, the test tool looks for the file named `xxx_test.go`. Note that each test function takes the `T` pointer argument, which provides the useful methods for test control. By the `T` struct pointer, the status of the test could be set. For instance, the methods `Fail` and `FailNow`, cause the test to fail. With the help of the `T` struct pointer, the test could be skipped by calling `Skip`, `Skipf`, or `SkipNow`.

The interesting method of the `T` pointer is the method `Helper`. By calling the method `Helper`, the current function is marked as the helper function, and if the `FailNow` (`Fatal`) is called within this function, then the test output points to the code line where the function is called within the test, as can be seen in the preceding sample code.

 Note that the `Log` method, (and its variants), are not visible if the test tool is not run in verbose mode (with –v flag), or if the particular test failed (this applies only for the `T` tests). Try to run this sample code without the –v flag.

See also

- The following recipe covers the basics of benchmarking
- For a more detailed description of the testing package, see the rich documentation of the testing package at `https://golang.org/pkg/testing`

Benchmarking the code

The previous recipe walks through the testing part of the testing package, and in this recipe, the basics of the benchmarking will be covered.

How to do it...

1. Open the console and create the folder `chapter11/recipe03`.
2. Navigate to the directory.

3. Create the file `sample_test.go` with the following content:

```go
package main

import (
  "log"
  "testing"
)

func BenchmarkSampleOne(b *testing.B) {
  logger := log.New(devNull{}, "test", log.Llongfile)
  b.ResetTimer()
  b.StartTimer()
  for i := 0; i < b.N; i++ {
    logger.Println("This si awesome")
  }
  b.StopTimer()
}

type devNull struct{}

func (d devNull) Write(b []byte) (int, error) {
  return 0, nil
}
```

4. Execute the benchmark by `go test -bench=.`
5. See the output in the Terminal:

How it works...

Besides the pure test support, the testing package also provides the mechanisms for measuring the code performance. For this purpose, the B struct pointer as the argument is used, and the benchmarking functions in the test file are named as BenchmarkXXXX.

The essential part of the benchmark function is the manipulation with the timer and usage of the loop iteration counter N.

As you can see, the timer is manipulated with the methods, Reset/Start/StopTimer. By these, the result of the benchmark is influenced. Note that the timer starts running with the beginning of the benchmark function and the ResetTimer function just restarts it.

The N field of B is the iteration count within the measurement loop. The N value is set to a value high enough to reliably measure the result of the benchmark. The result in the benchmark log then displays the value of iterations and measured time per one iteration.

See also

- The subsequent recipe shows how the subtests within the tests can be created
- For more options and information on benchmarking, take a look into the package documentation here: https://golang.org/pkg/testing

Creating subtests

In some cases, it is useful to create a set of tests that could have a similar setup or clean-up code. This could be done without having a separate function for each test.

How to do it...

1. Open the console and create the folder chapter11/recipe04.
2. Navigate to the directory.
3. Create the file sample_test.go with the following content:

```
package main

import (
  "fmt"
  "strconv"
  "testing"
)

var testData = []int{10, 11, 017}
```

```go
func TestSampleOne(t *testing.T) {
  expected := "10"
  for _, val := range testData {
    tc := val
    t.Run(fmt.Sprintf("input = %d", tc), func(t *testing.T) {
      if expected != strconv.Itoa(tc) {
        t.Fail()
      }
    })
  }
}
```

4. Execute the tests by `go test -v`.
5. See the output in the Terminal:

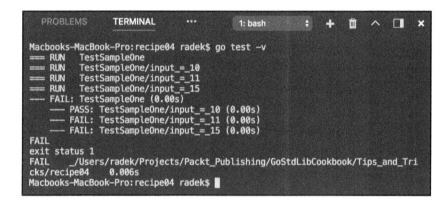

How it works...

The `T` struct of the `testing` package also provides the `Run` method that could be used to run the nested tests. The `Run` method requires the name of the subtest and the test function that will be executed. This approach could be beneficial while using, for example, the table driven tests. The code sample just uses a simple slice of `int` values as an input.

> The benchmarking struct `B`, also contains the same method, `Run`, which can provide a way of creating the subsequent steps of complex benchmarking.

See also

There is still much more to find out in the package documentation, `https://golang.org/pkg/testing`.

Testing the HTTP handler

The testing of the `HTTP` server could be complicated. The Go standard library simplifies this with a handy package, `net/http/httptest`. This recipe describes how to utilize this package to test the `HTTP` handlers.

How to do it...

1. Open the console and create the folder `chapter11/recipe05`.
2. Navigate to the directory.
3. Create the file `sample_test.go` with the following content:

```go
package main

import (
  "fmt"
  "io/ioutil"
  "net/http"
  "net/http/httptest"
  "testing"
  "time"
)

const cookieName = "X-Cookie"

func HandlerUnderTest(w http.ResponseWriter, r *http.Request) {
  http.SetCookie(w, &http.Cookie{
    Domain: "localhost",
    Expires: time.Now().Add(3 * time.Hour),
    Name: cookieName,
  })
  r.ParseForm()
  username := r.FormValue("username")
  fmt.Fprintf(w, "Hello %s!", username)
}
```

```go
func TestHttpRequest(t *testing.T) {

  req := httptest.NewRequest("GET",
                 "http://unknown.io?username=John", nil)
  w := httptest.NewRecorder()
  HandlerUnderTest(w, req)

  var res *http.Cookie
  for _, c := range w.Result().Cookies() {
    if c.Name == cookieName {
      res = c
    }
  }
  if res == nil {
    t.Fatal("Cannot find " + cookieName)
  }

  content, err := ioutil.ReadAll(w.Result().Body)
  if err != nil {
    t.Fatal("Cannot read response body")
  }

  if string(content) != "Hello John!" {
    t.Fatal("Content not matching expected value")
  }
}
```

4. Execute the test by `go test`.
5. See the output in the Terminal:

How it works...

For the testing of the `Handler` or `HandlerFunc`, the `net/http/httptest` could be leveraged. This package provides the struct `ResponseRecorder` that is able to record the content of the response and provide it back for asserting the values. For assembling the request, the `NewRequest` function of the `net/http` package is used.

 The `net/http/httptest` package also contains the version of the HTTP server which starts listening on the systems chosen port on the localhost. This implementation is intended to be used for end-to-end testing.

Accessing tags via reflection

The Go language allows the tagging of structured fields with additional information. This information is usually used as additional information for encoders, or any kind of additional processing of struct. This recipe will show you how to access these.

How to do it...

1. Open the console and create the folder `chapter11/recipe06`.
2. Navigate to the directory.
3. Create the file `structtags.go` with the following content:

```go
package main

import (
  "fmt"
  "reflect"
)

type Person struct {
  Name string `json:"p_name" bson:"pName"`
  Age int `json:"p_age" bson:"pAge"`
}

func main() {
  f := &Person{"Tom", 30}
  describe(f)
}
```

```go
func describe(f interface{}) {
  val := reflect.TypeOf(f).Elem()
  for i := 0; i < val.NumField(); i++ {
    typeF := val.Field(i)
    fieldName := typeF.Name
    jsonTag := typeF.Tag.Get("json")
    bsonTag := typeF.Tag.Get("bson")
    fmt.Printf("Field : %s jsonTag: %s bsonTag: %s\n",
               fieldName, jsonTag, bsonTag)
  }
}
```

4. Execute the code by `go run structtags.go`.
5. See the output in the Terminal:

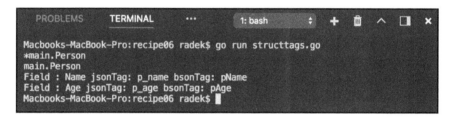

How it works...

The `struct` tags could be extracted with the use of the `reflect` package. By calling the `TypeOf`, we get the pointer `Type` for `Person`, subsequently, by calling the `Elem` we get the `Type` of the value which the pointer points to.

The resulting `Type` gives us access to the `struct` type `Person` and its fields. By iterating over the fields and retrieving the fields, by calling the `Field` method, we obtain the `StructField`. The `StructField` type contains the `Tag` field which provides access to the `struct` tags. The `Get` method on the `StructTag` field then returns the specific tag.

Sorting slices

The sorting of data is a very common task. The Go standard library simplifies the sorting by the sort package. This recipe gives a brief look at how to use it.

How to do it...

1. Open the console and create the folder `chapter11/recipe07`.
2. Navigate to the directory.
3. Create the file `sort.go` with the following content:

```
package main

import (
  "fmt"
  "sort"
)

type Gopher struct {
  Name string
  Age int
}

var data = []Gopher{
  {"Daniel", 25},
  {"Tom", 19},
  {"Murthy", 33},
}

type Gophers []Gopher

func (g Gophers) Len() int {
  return len(g)
}

func (g Gophers) Less(i, j int) bool {
  return g[i].Age > g[j].Age
}

func (g Gophers) Swap(i, j int) {
  tmp := g[j]
  g[j] = g[i]
  g[i] = tmp
}

func main() {

  sort.Slice(data, func(i, j int) bool {
    return sort.StringsAreSorted([]string{data[i].Name,
                        data[j].Name})
  })
```

```
fmt.Printf("Sorted by name: %v\n", data)

gophers := Gophers(data)
sort.Sort(gophers)

fmt.Printf("Sorted by age: %v\n", data)

}
```

4. Execute the code by `go run sort.go`.
5. See the output in the Terminal:

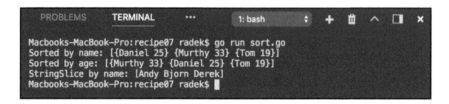

How it works...

The sample code shows both ways of how to comfortably sort a slice with the help of the `sort` package. The first approach is more ad hoc and it uses the `Slice` function of the `sort` package. The `Slice` function consumes the slice to be sorted and the so-called less function, which defines whether the element `i` should be sorted before element `j`.

The second approach requires more code and planning ahead. It leverages the `Interface` interface of the `sort` package. The interface acts as a representative of the data and requires it to implement essential methods on sorted data: `Len` (defines the amount of data), `Less` (less function), `Swap` (method called to swap the elements). If the data value implements this interface, then the `Sort` function of the `sort` package could be used.

The primitive type slices `float64`, `int`, and `string` are covered in the `sort` package. So, the existing implementation could be used. For example, to sort a slice of strings, the `Strings` function could be called.

Breaking HTTP handlers into groups

This recipe gives advice on how the HTTP handlers could be separated into modules.

How to do it...

1. Open the console and create the folder `chapter11/recipe08`.
2. Navigate to the directory.
3. Create the file `handlegroups.go` with the following content:

```go
package main

import (
  "fmt"
  "log"
  "net/http"
)

func main() {

  log.Println("Staring server...")
  // Adding to mani Mux
  mainMux := http.NewServeMux()
  mainMux.Handle("/api/",
  http.StripPrefix("/api", restModule()))
  mainMux.Handle("/ui/",
  http.StripPrefix("/ui", uiModule()))

  if err := http.ListenAndServe(":8080", mainMux); err != nil {
    panic(err)
  }

}

func restModule() http.Handler {
  // Separate Mux for all REST
  restApi := http.NewServeMux()
  restApi.HandleFunc("/users", func(w http.ResponseWriter,
                   r *http.Request) {
    w.Header().Set("Content-Type", "application/json")
    fmt.Fprint(w, `[{"id":1,"name":"John"}]`)
  })
  return restApi
}

func uiModule() http.Handler {
  // Separate Mux for all UI
  ui := http.NewServeMux()
  ui.HandleFunc("/users", func(w http.ResponseWriter,
                 r *http.Request) {
```

```
            w.Header().Set("Content-Type", "text/html")
            fmt.Fprint(w, `<html><body>Hello from UI!</body></html>`)
        })

        return ui
    }
```

4. Execute the code by `go run handlegroups.go`.

5. See the output:

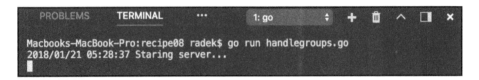

6. Access the browser URL `http://localhost:8080/api/users`, the output should look like this:

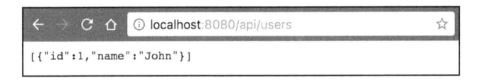

7. In the same way, you can test `http://localhost:8080/ui/users`:

How it works...

For separating the handlers into modules, the code uses the `ServeMux` for each module, (`rest` and `ui`). The handling of URLs for the given module is defined relatively. This means if the final URL for the `Handler` should be `/api/users`, then the defined path within the module would be `/users`. The module itself would be set to `/api/` URL.

The module is plugged into the main `ServeMux` pointer named `mainMux` by leveraging the `StripPrefix` function, which removes the module prefix. For instance, the REST module created by the `restModule` function, is plugged into the main `ServeMux` by `StripPrefix("/api",restModule())`. The handled URL within the module will then be `/users`, instead of `/api/users`.

Utilizing HTTP/2 server push

The HTTP/2 specification provides the server with the ability to push the resources, prior to being requested. This recipe shows you how to implement the server push.

Getting ready

Prepare the private key and self-signed X-509 certificate. For this purpose, the `openssl` utility could be used. By executing the command `openssl genrsa -out server.key 2048`, the private key derived with the use of the RSA algorithm is generated to file, `server.key`. Based on this private key, the X-509 certificate could be generated by calling `openssl req -new -x509 -sha256 -key server.key -out server.crt -days 365`. The `server.crt` file is created.

How to do it...

1. Open the console and create the folder `chapter11/recipe09`.
2. Navigate to the directory.
3. Create the file `push.go` with the following content:

```
package main

import (
  "io"
  "log"
  "net/http"
)

func main() {

  log.Println("Staring server...")
  // Adding to mani Mux
```

```go
http.HandleFunc("/",func(w http.ResponseWriter, r *http.Request){
  if p, ok := w.(http.Pusher); ok {
    if err := p.Push("/app.css", nil); err != nil {
      log.Printf("Push err : %v", err)
    }
  }
  io.WriteString(w,
    `<html>
      <head>
        <link rel="stylesheet" type="text/css" href="app.css">
      </head>
      <body>
        <p>Hello</p>
      </body>
    </html>`
  )
})
http.HandleFunc("/app.css", func(w http.ResponseWriter,
                r *http.Request) {
  io.WriteString(w,
    `p {
      text-align: center;
      color: red;
    }`)
})

if err := http.ListenAndServeTLS(":8080", "server.crt",
                                "server.key", nil);
err != nil {
  panic(err)
}

}
```

4. Start the server by `go run push.go`.

5. Open the browser and open the developer's tool in
   URL `https://localhost:8080` (see the `Push` as initiator for `app.css`):

100 ms	200 ms	300 ms	400 ms	500 ms	600 ms

Name	Status	Type	Initiator	Size	Time
localhost	200	docu...	Other	215 B	23 ms
app.css	200	styles...	Push / (index)	113 B	525 ms
favicon.ico	200	text/h...	Other	181 B	6 ms

How it works...

First, note that the HTTP/2 requires the secured connection. The server push is very simple to implement. Since Go 1.8, the HTTP package provides the `Pusher` interface, which could be used to `Push` the assets before they are required. If the client, usually browser, supports the HTTP/2 protocol and the handshake with the server is successful, the `ResponseWriter` in `Handler` or `HandlerFunc` could be cast to `Pusher`. The `Pusher` provides only the `Push` method. The `Push` method consumes the target (which could be the absolute path or absolute URL) to resource and `PushOptions`, which can provide the additional options (by default the nil could be used).

In the preceding example, look at the output of the developer's tool in the browser. The pushed resource has the Initiator column with the value, `Push`.

Other Books You May Enjoy

If you enjoyed this book, you may be interested in these other books by Packt:

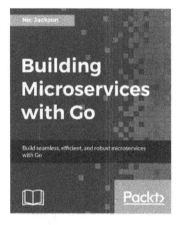

Building Microservices with Go

Nic Jackson

ISBN: 9781786468666

- Plan a microservice architecture and design a microservice
- Write a microservice with a RESTful API and a database
- Understand the common idioms and common patterns in microservices architecture
- Leverage tools and automation that helps microservices become horizontally scalable
- Get a grounding in containerization with Docker and Docker-Compose, which will greatly accelerate your development lifecycle
- Manage and secure Microservices at scale with monitoring, logging, service discovery, and automation
- Test microservices and integrate API tests in Go

Go Systems Programming

Mihalis Tsoukalos

ISBN: 9781787125643

- Explore the Go language from the standpoint of a developer conversant with Unix, Linux, and so on
- Understand Goroutines, the lightweight threads used for systems and concurrent applications
- Learn how to translate Unix and Linux systems code in C to Golang code
- How to write fast and lightweight server code
- Dive into concurrency with Go
- Write low-level networking code

Leave a review - let other readers know what you think

Please share your thoughts on this book with others by leaving a review on the site that you bought it from. If you purchased the book from Amazon, please leave us an honest review on this book's Amazon page. This is vital so that other potential readers can see and use your unbiased opinion to make purchasing decisions, we can understand what our customers think about our products, and our authors can see your feedback on the title that they have worked with Packt to create. It will only take a few minutes of your time, but is valuable to other potential customers, our authors, and Packt. Thank you!

Index

A

application
  shutting down 40, 43

B

binary data
  reading 149, 150
  writing 149
binary representation
  converting between 94

C

case
  controlling 70
charset
  reading 143
  writing 143
checksums
  generating 106, 109
child process
  information, retrieving 29, 32
  reading from 32, 39
  writing from 32, 39
code block
  executing 125
  executing, only once 278
code
  benchmarking 295, 296
  testing 293, 295
  with delay, executing 127, 129
complex numbers
  operating 101
connection
  validating 216, 218
content generated

  serving, with templates 260, 261
cookies
  handling 264, 267
CSV (comma-separated values)
  parsing 72, 75
current process PID
  obtaining 21, 22
current working directory
  retrieving 19, 20
customization
  logging 292, 293

D

data
  extracting, from incomplete JSON array 161
  retrieving, from query result 231, 234
date
  arithmetics 120
  converting, to epoch 117
  differences, spotting 122
  formatting, to string 113
  serializing 131
  string, parsing into 115
  time units, retrieving 119
DCL (Data Control Language) 221
DDL (Data Definition Language) 221
degrees
  and radians, converting between 103
directory
  creating 176
  listing 172, 174
DML (Data Modeling Language) 221

E

environment variables
  obtaining 15, 18

setting, with default values 15
setting, with default variables 18
epoch
    converting, to dates 117
errgroup
    used, for propagating errors 287, 289
errors
    propagating, with errgroup 287
    writing 137
external process
    calling 25, 28

F

fastest result
    obtaining, from multiple sources 285, 287
file listings
    filtering 178, 180
file permissions
    modifying 175, 176
file
    comparing 180, 183
    creating 176
    information, obtaining 166
    opening, by name 139, 141
    position, seeking 145, 148
    reading, into string 141
    writing 169
    writing, from multiple goroutines 170
flag package
    used, for creating program interface 12, 15
Float type
    reference 90
floating-point arithmetics
    handling 89, 90
floating-point numbers
    comparing 84, 86
    rounding 87, 88
form variables
    resolving 271
functional options
    using, with file configuration 43, 46
functions
    executing 241, 244

G

Golang version
    retrieving 8, 9
goroutines
    synchronizing, with WaitGroup 283

H

hexadecimal representation
    converting between 94
host addresses
    translating, to IP addresses 190
HTTP handler
    separating, into groups 304, 306
    testing 299, 301
HTTP headers
    reading 198
    writing 198
HTTP middleware layer
    creating 256, 258
HTTP redirects
    handling 200, 203
HTTP request
    creating 196, 198
    handling 254, 255
HTTP server
    connecting to 191, 194
    creating 252, 253
    graceful shutdown, implementing 267, 269
HTTP/2 server push
    utilizing 307, 309

I

incomplete JSON array
    data, extracting 161
IP addresses
    translating, into host addresses 190

J

JSON-RPC service
    calling 209, 211

L

local IP addresses
 resolving 186, 187
logarithms
 using 105, 106

M

map, for concurrent access
 creating 276, 278
map
 query result, parsing 234, 238
multiple clients
 handling 250, 252
multiple goroutines
 file, writing 170
 resources, pooling across 281, 283
multiple writers
 writing 151
Mutex
 used, for synchronizing access to resource 274

N

non-unicode charset
 string, decoding from 67, 69
numbers
 formatting 91, 94

O

objects
 serializing, to binary format 154, 156
octal representation
 converting between 94
operating system signals
 handling 22, 25

P

package testing
 reference 299
pending query
 canceling 225, 227
plurals
 formatting, in correct format 96, 98
PostgreSQL database

connecting to 214, 215
prepared statements
 using 221, 224
program arguments
 accessing 11
program interface
 creating, with flag package 12, 15

Q

query result
 data, retrieving 231, 234
 metadata, reading 228, 230
 parsing, into map 234, 238

R

random numbers
 generating 99, 101
redirects
 handling 262, 263
regex pattern
 used, for finding substring 65
remote server
 connecting 188, 190
resource access
 synchronizing, with Mutex 274
RESTful API
 consuming 203, 206

S

secured HTTP content
 serving 269, 271
separator
 used, for joining string slice 54, 56
simple email
 sending 206, 208
slices
 sorting 302, 304
standard input
 reading 134, 136, 137
standard output
 writing 137
statements
 executing 218, 221
static files

serving 258
stored procedures
  executing 241, 244
string slice
  joining, with separator 54, 56
string
  concatenating, with writer 57, 60
  converting, to numbers 82, 83
  date, formatting to 113
  decoding, from non-unicode charset 67, 69
  disintegrating, into words 50, 54
  parsing, into date 115
  substring, finding 48
  substring, replacing 62, 64
  whitespace, managing 76, 78
subsets
  creating 297
substring
  finding, in string 48
  finding, with regex pattern 65

T

tabwriter
  used, for aligning text 60
tags
  accessing, via reflection 301
TCL (Transaction Control Language) 221
TCP server
  creating 246, 247
templates
  used, for serving content generated 260, 261
temporary files
  creating 167
testing package
  reference 295
text document
  indenting 78
text
  aligning, with tabwriter 60

time package
  reference 115
time zones
  converting between 123
time
  serializing 131
timeout long-running operations
  implementing 129, 131
today's date
  finding 112
transactions
  handling 238, 241

U

URL
  building 195, 196
  parsing 195, 196
User Datagram Protocol (UDP) server
  creating 248, 249
user home directory
  resolving 183

W

WaitGroup
  used, for synchronizing goroutines 283
whitespace
  managing, in string 76, 78
writer
  and reader, piping between 152
  used, for concatenating string 57, 60

X

XML file
  parsing 159, 161

Z

ZIP files
  reading 156, 158
  writing 156, 158

www.ingramcontent.com/pod-product-compliance
Lightning Source LLC
Chambersburg PA
CBHW080621060326
40690CB00021B/4766